THE BUTCHER'S DAUGHTER

The Story of an Army Nurse with ALS

by Sandra Lesher Stuban, RN

"The Butcher's Daughter: The Story of an Army Nurse with ALS," by Sandra Lesher Stuban, RN. ISBN 978-1-60264-352-9.

Published 2009 by Virtualbookworm.com Publishing Inc., P.O. Box 9949, College Station, TX 77842, US. ©2009, Sandra Lesher Stuban, RN. All rights reserved. No part of this publication may be reproduced, stored in a retrieval system, or transmitted in any form or by any means, electronic, mechanical, recording or otherwise, without the prior written permission of Sandra Lesher Stuban, RN.

Manufactured in the United States of America.

This book is dedicated to
my parents
Robert and Lois Lesher
The Butcher and his wife

Acknowledgements

I must say special thanks to Karen Gausman, Susan Jackson, and Nancy Rosenfeld who reviewed my manuscript, offered sage advice, and encouraged me, telling me my story *must* be told and published. Here it is!

The Butcher's Daughter: The Story of an Army Nurse with ALS: Introduction

I am on a journey I never expected. I didn't ask to go on this journey nor did I do anything to instigate it. I am inviting you to join me. Though I made some mistakes along the way, I also made some good choices. Regardless, they are all learning experiences. Whatever your situation, whether you have ALS or another disability, are a health care provider, serve in the military, are someone facing a difficult time, or simply looking for an unusual story, I think you will be enlightened by my journey.

I will take you to my hometown in the rural mountains of central Pennsylvania where I grew up as a daughter of a butcher and learned a strong set of country-based values. At 17, I left the safety of this small town to attend nursing school in Philadelphia where I not only received an Ivy League education but also learned about being an independent young woman in a big city. I will share with you vignettes about my military career as an Army nurse in Hawaii as a Lieutenant with moves to Texas, Germany, the Midwest and back to Hawaii again, this time as a Lieutenant Colonel. Then I was hit with the devastating, show-stopping news—I had ALS.

My journey continues with ALS from being a strong and physically fit military officer to a ventilator-using quadriplegic and the effect the slowly progressing paralysis had on me, robbing me of my beloved nursing career and a normal family life, extinguishing my future plans. I will share with you my mental and emotional anguish on this hard road. Along the way I also made some important discoveries about life in general and asked tough questions of myself. Why am I here? What is my purpose? What is the meaning of my life? How can I accept my new life? I will take you with me from the lowest of lows to my eventual positive outlook.

Most importantly, I share specific advice I learned from first hand experience dealing with the devastation of ALS and from my experiences as a registered nurse. In the Lessons Learned sections at the end of each chapter starting with the diagnosis, I offer concrete, straightforward recommendations to help you avoid common pitfalls.

I am writing this book for anyone who has ever faced an unexpected, unwanted obstacle in their life, which I believe is everyone. I hope I can offer a different perspective and perhaps a different outlook on life's perplexing difficulties. And finally I hope I can encourage a new appreciation and respect for those who are physically impaired. So, buckle up, let's begin our journey.

Chapter 1
ALS the Thief

"I complained I had no shoes till I saw a man that had no feet."—Author Unknown

The thief is determined to destroy my life. But I am equally determined to persevere. It is known by many names—ALS, amyotrophic lateral sclerosis, motor neuron disease, Lou Gehrig's Disease. The thief took my strong, physically fit body and left it pilfered and quadriplegic. When I was diagnosed 14 years ago, I didn't know what to do, what to think, how to act, or how to adapt. Little did I know that my healthy years prepared me for this journey, this venture into the unknown world of ALS.

Initially I did not know what I was up against but over time I was able to successfully protect and prepare myself both physically and mentally. ALS assaults the motor neurons in the spinal cord and brain until they sclerose and die. The motor neurons are the nerve cells required to activate skeletal muscles. As ALS slowly progresses, the muscles become weaker and weaker until they no longer respond. Paralysis is the end result, paralysis of muscles needed to move, breathe, swallow, and speak. The interesting part of this is that only motor neurons are affected meaning that internal organs, sensation, bowel and bladder function, and mental ability are left unscathed.

Dr Jean Marie Charcot, a French neurologist, first described ALS in 1874. Surely, much progress has been made since then. But disappointingly, today scientists still do not know what causes ALS though many theories exist. Environmental factors are highly suspicious such as exposure to pesticides, lead, strenuous exercise, toxins, certain viruses, and even amalgam teeth fillings have been questioned. Interestingly several recent studies have identified military service as a risk factor. A Harvard study found that men with any military service had a nearly 60 percent greater risk of developing ALS than men with no service history. In addition, there is still no effective treatment available. The only drug approved by the FDA (Food and Drug Administration) for ALS, riluzole, extends life by a meager two to three months.

I am one of 30,000 Americans with ALS. Fifty percent of us will die within three years, 20 percent will live five years, and ten percent will live more than ten years. Most of us have sporadic ALS meaning it happens out of the clear blue, but ten percent have familial ALS where genes are passed on to the next generation.

Now wait a minute! I understand ALS causes complete paralysis in healthy people, there is no known cause, there is no effective treatment, there is no cure, and most will die in three years. There must be something positive among all this nastiness.

Research is more active today than it was 14 years ago when I was diagnosed. I follow the literature very closely. Today scientists and researchers are investigating gene therapy, nerve growth factors, glial cells, apotosis, and stem cells to mention a few areas of active study. The ALS Association is supporting the expedited use of drugs in human clinical trials that have been approved for other treatments and may show promise. This certainly gives us hope but the reality is that there is little progress in moving animal experiments from the lab to applications in humans for effective treatments for neurologists to prescribe. Even the most basic questions remain unanswered, such as How are motor neurons killed? and Why do only motor neurons die and not other nerves? In the meantime more and more fathers, mothers, sisters, brothers, and friends die every day from this dreaded disease.

When Lou Gehrig, the famous Yankee baseball player, was diagnosed in 1939 he succumbed to the thievery of ALS less than two years later. Advancements in health care allow those with the diagnosis to extend their lives amidst the ravages of ALS. People can live longer by choosing to use a feeding tube, noninvasive ventilation like bipap, and invasive ventilation using a tracheostomy and ventilator. However, five percent of folks with ALS choose to use a ventilator, the other 95 percent choose an early death usually from respiratory failure.

I have discovered that an essential part of surviving ALS is attitude. With such a devastating, horrific disease I had to pull myself up by my boot straps, take a serious look inside myself, make a decision about how much I wanted to fight, and then move on with the right attitude and ambitions. Reflecting on my life I see many values instilled during my childhood and experiences as a nurse and Army officer that prepared me for this journey. I am not a victim. I am not a prisoner. I am not without options. I didn't ask for ALS and I don't like it but I have figured out how to live successfully and meaningfully as a seriously disabled woman cohabitating with my nemesis ALS the thief.

Sandra, age 9, (center) with sisters Teresa and Sheila and their vizsla dog Penny, at home, Elizabethville, Pa.

Chapter 2
A Girl From Elizabethville

"It is not what you do for your children but what you have taught them to do for themselves that will make them successful human beings."—Ann Landers

I was known as the agitator and loved it. I had the ability to stir things up. I chased my two sisters with daddy-long-legs and caught honeybees in jars to taunt them but I was a good kid.

I grew up in the tiny town of Elizabethville in Lykens valley amid the mountains of central Pennsylvania. With about 1500 residents, E'ville had one red light at the square, two protestant churches, a bank, a veterinarian, a volunteer fire company, and a swimming pool. The closest fast food joint was a thirty-mile trek over Berry Mountain then Peters Mountain toward Harrisburg. Ethnic diversity was nonexistent—no blacks, no Hispanics, no Asians, no Jews, few Catholics, and a handful of Amish. The valley was white and protestant, that's just the way it was.

A mile north of town was Lesher's Meat, my Dad's butcher shop, providing an essential service to the local farmers. My grandfather Marlyn Lesher started the business during the Depression, Dad joined him while still in high school. They both were entrepreneurs, risk takers, and good and honest businessmen. Farm animals were delivered on the hoof to the holding pen and returned cut, wrapped, and frozen as steaks, roasts, hamburger, and whatever cuts the customer ordered.

We lived in a small cottage-like house that Dad and Pappy Lesher built on the edge of a grove of trees less than 100 feet from the butcher shop. Mom was busy raising us kids but she also worked with Dad and continued to do so through their 50+ years of marriage.

There were three of us, all girls, and I was the middle child, whatever that means. Teresa was three years older and Sheila was three years younger. We played well together, there was nobody else so we entertained ourselves with what we had. Dad had two trucks for transporting animals that were called the big cattle truck and the little cattle truck. When I saw Pappy Lesher getting into the little cattle truck I knew he was going to a local farm to pick up animals. "Can I go? Can I go? " The response was always "Go ask your mother." And off we went.

I also spent time in the butcher shop just checking things out. I was curious about everything. What are you doing? What's that? Where are the animals? Why, why, why? Mom would not allow us to watch the actual killing of the animals, at that time it was done with a rifle. But after the shot, Dad opened the door and my two sisters and I sat on three chairs Mom had set up for us. I watched it all and began to understand the natural phases of life. Meat for dinner didn't come from a grocery store, it came from a farm. Interestingly, but perhaps not unpredictably, all three of us girls later chose careers in health care.

I was also intrigued with other goings-on in the butcher shop. There were two huge 50 gallon kettles used for rendering lard, making scrapple, and cooking meat for holiday mince meat. I was too small to see inside so I was lifted up and allowed to help stir this giant pot. I wanted to help. In my travels exploring the shop, I discovered a barrel with a metal spout on top. I noticed that a drip of dark brown thick liquid occasionally fell from the spout. What could this possibly be? I watched, I moved closer, I caught a drop on my finger, and I cautiously put a bit on my tongue. I discovered a gold mine—a barrel of molasses used in the recipe to cure ham and bacon. I caught many drops of molasses over the years and never told a soul. When I was five we moved to the other side of town and sadly my spontaneous adventures to the butcher shop ended.

Robert Marlyn Lesher, my Dad, was a remarkable man. Through the years he taught me some pretty incredible values. I didn't learn them by sitting down and discussing philosophy, I learned from his example. He built and expanded his business through sheer hard work, intellectual calculations, and the desire to succeed. I saw him as a physically strong man with an ability to solve any problem, a profusion of common sense, and a bullish determination of his convictions. He was not someone to tangle with physically or mentally. Early on he had expectations of me that I never questioned. He gave me responsibilities that I always tried to fulfill, expected me to make right decisions and be accountable for my actions, instilled the idea that I should strive to be independent, and planted the ethos that I could do anything I set my mind to. It didn't matter that I was a girl and it didn't matter that I was from hicktown USA. This may seem like a pretty tall order for a kid but it's what I grew up with. It was no big deal.

I was not permitted to work while school was in session but when I was old enough, about 12, I worked summers with Dad. I sold beef and pork cuts behind a 45-foot long refrigerated meat case in Lewisburg, an hour to the north, and in Elizabethtown, an hour to the south. Dad was the epitome of quality customer service with just a bit of charisma. Dad spoke fluent Pennsylvania Dutch and delighted his customers with this touch of familiarity. I worked long hours, constantly on my feet, for more than 12 hours a day and was never paid monetarily for my work. I don't remember ever complaining about being tired or about the long hours. Dad set the example in working until all work was done. Period. I saw and practiced this work ethic. I was never afraid of hard work.

In 1961 when I was five, our family moved to a new house two miles west of Elizabethville that Dad built with the help of local artisans, friends, and his father-in-law Albert Hoke. Dad bought the farmland from a local farmer and turned a field into our ranch-style home. The backyard, with wheat fields on one side and corn on the other, gently sloped down about 300 feet where Berry Mountain began its rise.

Penny, a vizla pointer hunting dog, joined our family. She was a beautiful shorthaired, bronze bundle of energy that Dad used to hunt ring-neck pheasants and to keep the groundhogs in check. But Penny was one of the girls too. She did everything with my sisters and I. We often played in the mountain, frequently visiting the grove of coniferous trees called Pine Tree Castle, halfway up the mountain. When it was time to go home Dad did his two fingered whistle and the four of us ran all the way home.

I truly believed Penny loved us despite our antics, I think she even laughed with us. We put boots on her four feet and watched her walk awkwardly while we rolled on the floor in hysterics. We also painted her toenails, put peanut butter on the roof of her mouth, and took her sledding down the backyard hill. She was definitely part of the family.

Teresa, Sheila, and I played hard and worked hard together. Teresa was a small, short, quiet kid and even though she was three years older, I was as tall as her. Sheila was three years younger and Teresa and I let her tag along. We were never bored. There was always something to do in the yard like killer badminton or crochet. At the creek at the foot of the mountain we built tiny boats made of leaves and twigs then raced them through the water. In the mountain we explored and made up games. We had roller skates, the kind that attached to your shoes, and we skated on the sidewalks around the house and the open carport making up crazy rules to crazy games. Down the backyard hill in the next field was Botts' pond where we ice skated every winter. During bad weather we were known to play marathon games of Monopoly that sometimes lasted for days. But Mom always had "jobs" for us to do too like picking stones, sweeping the sidewalks, weeding the garden, cleaning out the dishwasher, hanging the wash outside on the washline, and lots more.

Somehow I was always in the thick of things stirring up trouble. I didn't think I was a troublemaker but whatever I did certainly didn't meet Mom's strict rules for proper conduct. One of Mom's favorite punishments for bad behavior when I was still a kid was the chair. Removed from the site of the infraction, I had to sit in a chair away from the fun until the buzzer on the stove went off. Soon I figured out that I could remain seated and bounce the chair up and down toward the fun. I quickly learned that this was not tolerated either. As a teen I tested Mom's patience and limits with my assertions to be independent. I wanted to know why she made certain decisions and when I didn't get a reasonable explanation in my eyes I was perturbed.

Lois Hoke Lesher, my Mom, ran the house with an iron fist and a watchful eye. Her job of raising three girls, especially when we were all teenagers at the same time, was certainly unenviable. She had high expectations, insisted on cleanliness and orderliness, had an unstoppable energy level, and was completely devoted to

Dad. One of her favorite sayings was "The way you make your bed is the way you have to sleep in it."

Mom was responsible for introducing me to the artistic and cultural side of living, as much as was available in our area. When there was no girl scout leader she assumed the role so all girls in the community could benefit. When the children's choir in church needed a director she came forward and again answered the call. Mom's example of volunteerism to improve the status quo was deeply implanted in my thinking.

I spent every summer day at the E'ville pool. As a kid I quickly passed all levels of swimming lessons. Later I taught swimming lessons and eventually took the new advanced lifeguard course organized and taught by Dee Marra at the E'ville pool. Dee volunteered to do this when she recognized the need and the benefit to the community. Her approach, conviction, and teaching style left a lasting impression on me that I tried to model. Although I was a strong swimmer and earned my certification, I only worked occasionally as a lifeguard because my priorities were always with Dad's business.

Although we always worked hard we did take memorable family vacations. My favorites were our weekend trips to my uncle Vernon Lesher's cottage on the Susquehanna River at Peach Bottom. The cottage was definitely rustic but at least it had running water, however the bathroom was an outhouse out back. The river made me an even stronger swimmer but the best thing was my uncle's boat. I learned to water ski here with Dad as my teacher. He built homemade skis and, being a strong swimmer himself, taught me how to ski. He was a firm but patient instructor. And at my first try, unable yet to judge the strength of the pull of the boat, I simply lost the hand grip. But he swam after me, helped me back into position, waited for the boat to realign, and continued his positive instruction. After that it only took a few more times to learn the precise timing and balance to succeed. I loved Peach Bottom and I loved water skiing with Dad's homemade skis.

When I was seven I started taking piano lessons from Gloria Ziegler, I continued for ten more years. Of course, like most kids, I didn't appreciate these instructions until many years later. Every year Gloria would organize a recital to showcase her pupils. The novices played first followed by the more experienced with the best student always playing last. I was definitely a novice when I participated in my first recital. I was amazed by the ability and talent I saw and heard. I didn't know the last person to play though I knew her name was Maxine. She was great. I thought to myself "What do I have to do to be that good?" Many years later in the last recital I participated in I was listed as the "last person" and realized my goal. I played Polonaise in A Flat by Chopin, a difficult and challenging piece, with perfection and received a standing ovation. I finally made it, I was good.

When I was 15 Gloria asked if I would be the accompanist for a contemporary Christian musical she was directing called "Life." She assembled her troupe of talented young people and called us the "New Life Singers." The performance was so powerful that other churches in Dauphin County invited us to perform. As word continued to spread, we traveled more frequently and further away. Gloria always believed in my abilities and my potential, and pushed me to higher and higher levels. I was no longer your run-of-the-mill rogue piano player, I had become a pianist with finesse and flair.

Church involvement was a significant part of growing up. St John's Lutheran church, also known as the Hill church, was founded in 1780 on a knoll surrounded by fields and farms between the towns of Elizabethville and Berrysburg. The red brick, three-story church had a tall 20-foot high white spire that could be seen for miles.

Interestingly, the original 40-foot spire was struck by lightning and eventually replaced with the "shorter" steeple. The entry level contained the Sunday school rooms and social hall, two large curved staircases led to the second floor sanctuary, and the balcony held the pipe organ, choir section, and additional pews. Mom made sure we didn't miss a Sunday or special event. I was baptized and confirmed here, took my first communion, served as acolyte, elected as a youth group officer, and was an accompanist for the children's choir. My faith was a no-nonsense type of affair with emphasis on moral, Christ-like living. The church provided the impetus, it was vibrant and alive with good deeds.

When I was about 15, Ray Matter, a life long member of the church and local farmer known for his incredible baritone, asked if I would serve as accompanist for his singing family. Ray and his five children were known throughout the valley for their harmony and unique presentation of Christian songs but no one in his family could play the piano. I accompanied them to all their singing engagements for many years and honed my musical skills.

St John's church had a distinctive pipe organ with two keyboards and 32 pipes ranging in size from 42 inches to the largest ones being six feet tall. The music produced by this colossal instrument was unbelievable. Kate Koppenhaver was the church organist forever, at least that's how it seemed to me—actually it was 28 years. She was a kindly gray haired lady who approached me suggesting we perform piano-organ duets for the Sunday services. This was actually quite an impressive production with the organ in the balcony in the rear, the piano in the front, and the congregation in the middle. We practiced and performed many duets together and became friends. While I was young and feisty at 15 and she was an unhurried 73 year old elder, we shared a common interest and talent in our music.

One evening I received a call that Kate was involved in a minor car accident and died the next night at home in her sleep. I was stunned, we had just practiced together the evening before on a duet for Sunday's service. I cried and cried, she was my friend. The church Council asked if I would serve as church organist. I wanted to do it but I knew it was a big commitment—every Sunday service, every special service, weekly prelude and postlude music selections, choir practice, and more. My biggest concern was that I didn't know how to play an organ and I didn't want to do anything but my best. There was no easing into this slowly, Kate was gone and I was the new organist. I asked Gloria to give me a crash course in Organ 101. I found it exhilarating, I was making music with one hand on one keyboard, another hand on another keyboard, and both feet going crazy on the pedals. I spent hours and hours practicing to learn the feel of this new instrument. I liked it and quickly mastered the challenge.

Another concern I had was that the congregation would not accept me, my style, or my selections. I knew Kate was conservative and everyone was comfortable with her musical temperment. I was 15 with a bounce in my step. While I respected Kate's style and interpretation of the music she played, it wasn't me. I wanted to use this organ to its fullest potential which I believed was untapped. I selected unique and unusual tones using the 32 different organ stops, I opened the pipes and let the full sound of the music fill the sanctuary, and I introduced the congregation to the great works of the classical masters like Bach, Mozart, Handel, Pachelbel, and more. What I discovered was not only did they accept me, they embraced me. They chuckled with me that I sure knew how to clean the spider webs out of the pipes. I truly loved playing this organ. I served as organist until I left the valley to attend nursing school.

The area high school for the surrounding small towns was located in Elizabethville. School buses traversed the farmlands of upper Dauphin County twice a day to get us to our appointments with education on time and home again. My bus driver was a dairy farmer who made his contribution to our education in this small but significant way. Upper Dauphin Area High School offered a basic, no-frill, no college AP education for the 400 students in grades 9 to 12. We could choose between one of three tracks—college prep or academic, commercial with emphasis on typing, shorthand, and stenography, or agriculture. The school acknowledged the traditional holidays plus we never had school the first day of deer season. Nobody I knew smoked, drank alcohol, used drugs, or got pregnant. Even though hunting rifles were common, we had no violence or disciplinary problems.

School sports kept us busy after school and on weekends. Without a hangout and no place to get a burger and soda with friends, we just went home. I had a few boyfriends but nobody that kept my interest. The most common date was going to the drive-in movie at Halifax ten miles away on the other side of Berry Mountain. But this wasn't much fun because we had to leave before the end of the first movie so I would be home by Mom's unbendable curfew. And of course proms were big events starting in junior high.

I was a mediocre student getting mostly A's and B's and some C's and was always looking for extracurricular activities to keep me busy. I was involved with the school chorus, sang with several special singing groups, and was one of several accompanists for these groups. Although I was more than capable, I was frequently given fewer and less difficult pieces as compared to my classmates who would be pursuing careers in music. I was frustrated that my potential, drive, and desire were not recognized and used. I guess it was fair but at the time I wanted more.

I had similar success with other extracurricular electives. I tried out for the girl's softball team but I was terrible. I tried out for the girl's basketball team with the same result. I tried out for the school play but not selected. I joined the gymnastic club but was marginal. Fortunately in my senior year, a girl's track team was formed, I finally found my niche. I was selected to run the 220, the 440, and throw the shotput. The running distances were grueling especially the 440 which was equivalent to sprinting a quarter mile. I often pushed myself so hard that I felt like my lungs were on fire and would throw up along the side of the track. But the shotput was a natural for me and I won many first places for the team.

I felt stifled by my high school education. I can look back and see the gaps that should have pushed me and challenged me and stimulated my mind. In school I never read a novel or classic, we never debated current affairs, we never discussed the Vietnam War, Watergate, or the resignation of our president. What was lacking in my basic education in the '70s, I made up for later, and then some.

Mr. Updegrove and Mr. Hives were the most eccentric yet most effective teachers I had in high school. Mr. U, a bald-headed short muscled fire plug type, taught English and frequently stressed his point on a dry subject by jumping on his desk and shouting questions to the class. Mr. Hives, whose classroom was across the hall from Mr. U, taught biology and chemistry. Mr. Hives, who had the wild look of a mad scientist, had a unique style of teaching, took the class on frequent field trips, and was always looking for unusual lab experiences. For one lab Dad dropped off a large stainless steel tray filled with the innards of a sheep he had butchered. Mr. Hives led the class in tracing the gastro-intestinal tract from esophagus to anus and identifying the major organs. This was just one example of how he tried to spark our interests in a topic he felt such a passion.

I believed Mr. Updegrove and Mr. Hives were in cahoots with each other because one or the other frequently would enter the other's classroom and stir up trouble. They seemed to know how to keep a class of 16 year olds interested and involved. I learned the most from these two unconventional scholars.

I graduated with 109 classmates in 1974. There was no recognition, no award, no acknowledgement. I received my diploma and was ready to move on. I was glad high school was finally over.

I always wanted to be a nurse but I also practically considered other service professions like pharmacist, physical therapist, and veterinarian. Nursing always won the internal debate. Then I thought through the financial impact of my education knowing Mom and Dad were fiscally vigilant. So I chose to pursue nursing through a three-year hospital diploma program which was significantly less expensive than a university education. I applied to hospital programs in Harrisburg, Lancaster, and York but their responses all indicated they were either downsizing or closing in the near future. This was the trend at the time.

I applied to one more school—the Hospital of the University of Pennsylvania (HUP) School of Nursing in Philadelphia. I was accepted and immediately responded I was coming. Some time later I unexpectedly received a letter saying I was eligible to apply for a scholarship based on the "whole" person not just grades or financial need. I was thrilled but not optimistic. I completed the application, listed my references as Mr. Updegrove and Mr. Hives, and wrote the required essay. I had to address my contribution to my community, my church, and my family, and why I wanted to be a nurse. As a 17 year old, I wrote the following about why I wanted to be a nurse:

> *"I enjoy giving and sharing life. Both create a sense of joy which starts within me and radiates outward to the people around me. I love living! Happiness is a real part of my life which I want to share with everyone. Many people are not as fortunate as myself in respect to my physical and mental health. I would generously help such underprivileged people to overcome their physical disabilities and to enjoy life with a smile. I need an occupation that satisfies me, nothing for glory or for money. This is what is wrong with society, too much concern for material goods instead of the emotional goods that we really should help sharing such as love, caring, and consideration. I achieve my satisfaction in nursing by knowing I am needed and by helping someone who needs me. By doing this I am not only helping the patient but I am also helping myself. I want to do something constructive in my life and for society. The only way to achieve all these goals in my mind is to be a well educated nurse."*

So I waited and the letter finally arrived. I was selected as a finalist and had an appointment for an interview before their scholarship board. Dad and I drove the three hours to Philadelphia. He dropped me off at the campus of the University of Pennsylvania and said he would pick me up later. I entered the Nursing Education Building not knowing where to go and what to expect but I asked questions and arrived to the interview anteroom well before my scheduled appointment. There were about 20 other girls there, all had a parent with them. This didn't bother me a bit, Dad trusted my independence and responsibility and I reveled in it.

I sat and watched and considered my strategy. After what seemed an eternity, my name was called and I entered the conference room. Around the long table were several female nursing faculty and one distinguished-looking older gentleman who I later learned was the person making this scholarship available. I was terribly nervous, not because I was in front of these important people, I was comfortable playing piano and organ for large audiences. I was nervous because of the magnitude and impact of the outcome. I sat at the end of the table and answered their questions with confidence and my usual high-spirited enthusiasm. I was eventually dismissed feeling pretty good but in reality having absolutely no idea how I stood against the others. I had never done anything like this before in my life.

I met up with Dad as we had arranged and asked him how he spent the hours while I was having my scholarship interview. He told me he went to a local Italian restaurant and ate ravioli. I chuckled to myself and told him about my interview.

Again I waited for a letter and when it arrived I learned I was the recipient of the Thomas B. McCabe scholarship. This was a full scholarship to pay for my entire nursing education provided by the distinguished gentleman who had experienced first hand the excellence of HUP nurses.

Being selected for this scholarship changed me. Even though I grew up in an extremely rural area and was a butcher's daughter, I competed against hotshot city and suburban kids and won. I won!

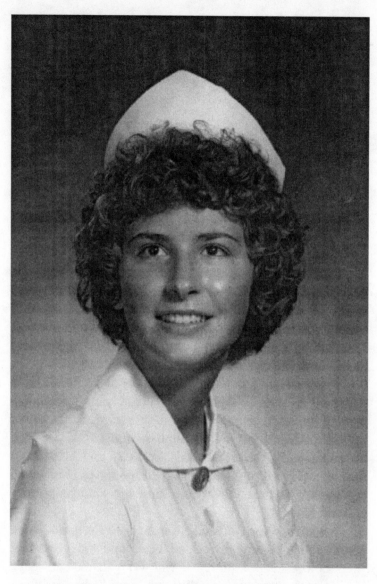

Sandra Stuban, 1977 Graduation, School of Nursing, Hospital of the University of Pennsylvania

Chapter 3
A Philadelphia Education

"Develop a passion for learning. If you do, you'll never cease to grow."—Anthony J. D'Angelo

I arrived with everything I would need to begin the next phase of my life—clothes, enthusiasm, and 17 years worth of values and principles from Dad and Mom. I knew I was in store for more than an education in nursing. I was taking a gigantic step going from a rural high school to a famous big city nursing school. I was ready.

I was assigned to King's Court, the dorm for all HUP (Hospital of the University of Pennsylvania) freshmen nursing students, connected by a courtyard to the newer upperclassmen dorm called English House. Some of the nursing faculty were there this first day and helped me find my assigned room and assigned roommate. I received my books, my class schedule, and my student nurse's uniform and cap.

It was time for Dad and Mom to head for home, there wasn't much to say, it had all been said the years and years before. Dad admitted it was very difficult to leave me in the heart of Philadelphia and Mom had tears in her eyes. Now they had to trust in everything they had taught me. But I was ecstatic about meeting my next challenge—the challenge of becoming a nurse.

Benjamin Franklin founded the University of Pennsylvania in 1740 giving it the distinction of being America's first university along with providing our country's first medical school and first teaching hospital. The 262-acre campus was located in west Philadelphia just west of the Schuykill River. Following the traditions and excellence of this Ivy League institution, the Hospital of the University of Pennsylvania (HUP) School of Nursing opened in 1886, providing one of the first formal "training" programs for nurses.

The School of Nursing operated in relative autonomy from the University—the King's Court and English House dorms housed only HUP nursing students, the HUP faculty taught only HUP nursing students, and the classes held in the Nursing Education Building on campus were open only to HUP nursing students. We were isolated in a way from the other university students but this separation had definite advantages.

That first day I looked over my class schedule. In a typical week in my first semester I had classes three days from 8 a.m. to 5 p.m. and clinicals two days from 7 a.m. to 4 p.m.. All classes and clinicals were mandatory, there was no time for electives, obviously. This was total immersion in learning nursing—breathing, sleeping, and dreaming about nursing. I knew about some students who chose to go to college to take an occasional afternoon class, go to parties, and learn to drink. I could not imagine this kind of mentality in nursing school, clearly this kind of student didn't go to this nursing school.

That first week many classmates quit, some even on the first day, and the three males in my class all quit too. We started with 128 students in my class and three years later 72 of us graduated.

That first day I also checked out my student nurse's uniform and cap. The uniform was a pale blue A-line shift with white cuffs on the short sleeves and a white collar.

The simple winged cap displayed freshman, junior, or senior status—plain white was worn by freshmen, one pale blue stripe across the wing was worn by juniors, and two stripes were reserved for seniors. We wore the uniform and cap with pride, this was obviously before nurses rebelled against the stigma of white uniforms and caps. We were recognized and respected throughout campus and the hospital. The HUP nurses' reputation preceded us.

The very first class was a welcome by the school's Director Iris Machlan Gross accompanied by her staff in the auditorium in the Nursing Education Building. She began by calling our names in alphabetical order—Miss So-and-so, Miss So-and-so... Miss Lesher. I stood up as those had done before me, she eyeballed me, gave a slight nod, then called the next name. I had never been called Miss Lesher in my life but that was to be my name for the next three years. I believed this was part of the transition I would make toward becoming a professional nurse. I also realized there was no anonymity in our numbers, every faculty member knew every student.

Ms Gross continued her welcome by telling us the school's history, legacy, reputation, and traditions. We were expected to conduct ourselves as young ladies and maintain an appropriate appearance at all times. Tardiness, absences, and sleeping in class were absolutely not tolerated and could result in expulsion. She said some of our classmates had already quit, more would quit, and even more would be asked to leave. She was pleased with the attrition because it further defined the eliteness and excellence HUP nurses were known for. Not just anyone could be a HUP nurse. She concluded with her famous quip. She expected that we were experiencing butterflies about what was expected of us but by the time we approached graduation these butterflies would be flying in formation.

I walked back to the dorm thinking about everything she said. I always welcomed a challenge and I was never afraid of hard work, I had no doubt I would pass the high standards this school expected. I was not a quitter.

The friends I made in these early days remained loyal to the end. Diane Jennings was from Long Island and later became my roommate for two years when we moved to English House. Sue Knetz was from New Jersey and Sandy Stilp was from Wilkes-Barre. The four of us endured the ups and downs together and we supported each other through all the stress and pressure of the three years ahead of us

We had housemothers at our dorms 24/7. These middle-aged women were the protectors for about 300 female nursing students. Believe me, others on campus knew where we were. But the housemothers were also enforcers. There were rules to be followed. The outside doors were locked at midnight every night and we had to knock to be let in if we were late as they glared disapprovingly. All guests had to sign in with them. And male guests were allowed visitation during certain hours on Saturday and Sunday only. Of course they also investigated loud and rowdy behavior in our rooms. All this didn't bother me in the least. I felt safe, it was almost like living at home with Mom's rules. Almost.

Clinicals started early in our schedule and were such an important part of our education. The orientation to clinicals was simply scary. The day before clinicals we were expected to go to our assigned unit where our patient assignment would be posted and read our patient's chart from beginning to end. Of course this included taking notes on everything not understood, which in the beginning was just about everything. Then we were expected to look up everything and make sense of it. And of course a careplan was required for every patient. Frequently preparation for clinicals ran late into the night, it was completely unheard of to go to clinicals without knowing answers to all questions.

The school's philosophy was that nursing could only be taught from a book to a certain extent, the more appropriate venue for this hands-on profession was with patients. Many people erroneously equated this type of program with free labor for the hospital. What a misstatement. The hospital was our classroom.

One clinical instructor oversaw only six students. We were constantly quizzed either one-on-one or in our small group so we learned from each other as well. These were short oral responses or informal presentations to the real life situations of patient care not a regurgitation from a page of a book. Preparation required independent self-driven study and research to be completely ready for clinicals. Being unprepared was never an option, the clinical instructors were tough, hard as nails, intolerant of mediocrity, and seemingly omnipotent.

The last part of the orientation was a physical tour of HUP showing us all the locations we would eventually learn clinical nursing. We stopped on Maloney 3 (that is Maloney building, 3rd floor). We paused outside a room where a nursing student was caring for her patient. I watched her, I knew she was a senior by the two stripes on her cap, and I was awed by her confidence and expert manner. I thought to myself "What do I have to do to be this good?"

And so I started learning nursing, every moment of every day. There was time for nothing else. Miss Arlene Hartung, the deputy Director, taught Med-Surg I, the fundamentals, the foundations, the basics to build our nursing education on. She was small in stature but big on perfection. She always taught in her white starched uniform and cap. Every T had to be crossed and every I had to be dotted. Sloppiness was never tolerated in our practice, our conduct, and our appearance. She physically checked for appropriate hairstyles, suitable jewelry, clean fingernails, and polished shoes. Mistakes were unacceptable and doing things right the first time were expected. Her persistence with always expecting high standards helped solidify our journey toward quality and excellence in our nursing practice. There was no other way.

In one of our first classes we watched a movie showing us how to give a bed bath. We looked at each other and snickered to ourselves thinking this was a fairly simple and mundane start to our exposure to patient care. Boy, were we wrong. A bath was not a two-minute splish splash deal. It was an opportunity for a complete assessment and so began our lessons in multitasking—washing, looking, feeling, smelling, talking all at the same time with 100 percent accuracy.

The first year flew by. I learned a new way to learn, a new way to study, and a new way to think. It was hard, very hard. There didn't seem to be enough hours in a day to do everything. The expectations were so high, the standards unbelievable but I felt the passion, the desire. I knew I was doing the right thing.

The second year expanded our patient care exposure to specialty areas. During my obstetric clinical rotation I saw my first delivery. I couldn't contain my tears. I had just witnessed a miracle, a mystery, a life entering life. I was just 18 and matured greatly that day. I didn't know what my clinical instructor would think of me, I was supposed to be professional. But she glanced at me and gave a slight smile, she understood the marvel of birth, it was her passion.

My psychiatric clinical was very different, it was the only venue off Penn's campus. The site was the State Psychiatric Hospital in New Castle, Delaware. We arrived Sunday evenings and returned to English House Friday evenings. We lived in dorms on-site Monday through

Friday in a secure section of the grounds. There were buildings for the criminally insane, long-term care, acute care, autistic children, and more. Again we were totally immersed into a different type of nursing care of the mentally ill. Frankly I was initially frighten of what I saw—wandering people, people with repetitive motions, people with empty eyes, people with unpredictable verbal and physical outbursts, and so much more. Our clinicals were never about standing back and observing, we were always involved with hands-on care and interventions. And so I again saw things I never experienced before in my naïve life in Elizabethville. Diseases of the mind were prevalent. Honestly this was one clinical I was happy to finish.

The pediatric clinical was done at CHOP, Children's Hospital of Philadelphia, located beside HUP. It seemed that every time I turned around I was exposed to something new and often disturbing, but this was part of my education. Every day I spent with these little patients and their parents embedded in my mind the vital importance and influence nurses have on the sick and their families.

Weekends were recovery time. About once a month I traveled by train from Philadelphia's 30th Street Station to Harrisburg where Dad and Mom picked me up. I was reinfused with Mom's cooking, sleep, and money to get me through until the next reprieve.

My roommate Diane rarely spent a weekend in the dorm. She either took the train south to Washington, DC to her fiancé attending Georgetown University or she took the train north to her home in Long Island. I went with her several times to New York, she acted as my guide when she took me into Manhatten. For the first time I saw the Statue of Liberty, the Empire State Building, the stock exchange, and traveled to the top floor of the World Trade Center. I was impressed to say the least.

Making it to senior year definitely meant I made the cut. Obviously the workload didn't change but I now knew the rules, standards, and expectations and I knew better how to prepare for all my assignments.

Two of my clinicals in my last year included critical care and team leading. Team leading was essentially being charge nurse and as a nursing student it meant being responsible for a team of patients, giving assignments to staff nurses, and troubleshooting any problems. Even though I had no formal class called Leadership it was integrated into every class, every clinical, and everything I did. We were expected to be leaders.

On one "recovery" weekend I was staying in the dorm I noticed a flyer posted on the main bulletin board in the lobby. The housemothers, of course, approved all postings for the bulletin board from around campus. This one was an invitation to a party at Drexel University just down the street. So Sue and I decided to check it out. We met two guys who definitely showed an interest—Dave, a civil engineering student at Drexel, had his eye on me and his roommate John, an electrical engineering student had his eye on Sue. And so started the courtships. Eventually I lost interest in Dave and eventually Sue and John got married.

As we neared graduation the class was expected to form committees to begin planning the traditional senior events—the senior brunch, the senior dinner dance, and the yearbook. Just about every class member participated in some way, this was really important to us. I served as co-editor for the yearbook and when a chorus of my classmates was formed to sing at graduation I was their accompanist.

Ms. Gross, the school's Director, sent a memo to each of us saying a tradition of the school was to have a student commencement address at graduation. A competition would be held for those interested in submitting speeches. I must have been nuts, maybe sleep deprived, but I decided to enter the competition. I had exams to study for, clinicals to prepare for, careplans to do, and papers to write. It wasn't like I didn't have enough to do but I wrote my speech and submitted it to the competition. I didn't know how many others did the same, maybe four or five. Later I was notified that my speech was selected for the student commencement address.

The next competition was to select the student to deliver my speech. I was not comfortable with public speaking (yet) and did not compete. I allowed a classmate to do the honors.

In one of my senior level classes, a guest was invited to talk about our future. She was a HUP recruiter. We would soon graduate and she wanted us to consider employment at HUP. HUP graduates were highly desirable because we knew the hospital, we knew the system, and we were simply the best nurses. Then she said something that had my complete attention. Because of the hospital's respect and appreciation of our excellence they had an education benefit that was only available to HUP graduates who chose to work at HUP. They would pay all costs to finish requirements for our BSN (Bachelor of Science in Nursing) at the University of Pennsylvania. They would pay for two courses three semesters each year while working full time at HUP. I couldn't believe it. Here was an opportunity for a fully funded degree from Penn and all I had to do was work hard. What a joke, I'd worked hard my whole life. I signed up.

Graduation day finally arrived. English House was a beehive of activity. Emotions ran high—we had all just completed the three most intense years of our lives. We knew no one could truly understand the strength and power of a HUP education except a fellow HUP graduate.

We met in our dorm's lobby dressed in our white starched graduation uniform, white stockings, white shoes, and the school's distinctive cap. Our housemothers beamed with pride and a few selected faculty tried to put order to our masses. I believed they were as excited as we were. The air was simply electric. When we were assembled in alphabetical order it was time to go. All 72 of us walked in single file from English House at 36th and Chestnut to Irvine Auditorium at 34th and Spruce in the center of campus. Cars stopped and people clapped and I heard someone ask "What's going on?" "The nurses are graduating."

All my guests who attended my graduation were already seated along with everybody else's guests. Irvine Auditorium was packed. As we entered in single file we received a standing ovation until the last person arrived to her seat. Then every single faculty member entered dressed in white uniform and cap, of course. We applauded them vigorously, we gave them credit for transforming us from motley kids into professional nurses. Ms. Gross, the Director, spoke and concluded by saying our butterflies now flew in formation. After the commencement address from the Dean of the School of Medicine, the student commencement address I had written was delivered by my classmate Denise. Written at the age of 20, this is the speech I wrote called Yesterday, Today, and Tomorrow.

"Yesterday, how long ago it seems! We were introduced into a new setting, a new environment—a new profession. We were taken from our secure homes and families and placed, by choice, into a new situation—that of nursing. With this transition, almost three years ago, we experienced our first taste of independence and real responsibility. And as a result we grew,

made new friends, and matured. These past three years are now only memories for us, whether they be of happiness, sadness, indifference, or a combination of all three. WOW! Those times went so fast. But at the time, they seemed to go so slow—counting off the months then the weeks then finally the days. And for some of us even the hours, until...

Today! It's here!! This day—the common goal we have all been striving for that once looked so far away—it was almost unreachable. But now what? Where did all that time go, the time that used to drag on and on? We, as a class unit, are experiencing our last moments together, here, right now! All the good and bad times of our three years of living together have finally peaked. And all the time we spent in preparation for this one day are becoming worthwhile and reality—sitting here in our graduation whites without a hair out of place. From this day on we will be granted, again, a new sense of independence and responsibility as was experienced those three short years ago. Today is extremely significant in each of our lives and no wonder! We will all experience that surge of adrenaline shooting through our bodies as our names are called one by one and as we proceed, singly, on stage to receive that piece of paper we've been striving and yearning for so hard these past years. We've got what we have waited for—but now what?!

Tomorrow. It's a new day! A different day! A day to do as I want. The decision is mine. We will each take a step ahead—but those steps will all be in different directions, at different paces, and with different goals. We have a new life ahead of us now, to mold into the lifestyle suitable to each. For we all have a unique and different concept of the type of nurse we have always wanted to be. This is our opportunity to pursue that dream which has finally come true. However, through the pursuit of this goal, our oneness will scatter, our adventures together cease, and our thoughts and memories of yesterday and today fade but never die."

This was the most important event in my life so far. As a new nurse I felt confident but not arrogant, cocksure but not cocky, assertive but not aggressive or passive. The terms burnout and reality shock meant nothing to me, the patient and the hospital had been my classroom and I was comfortable there.

I started work the Monday after graduation assigned to Ravdin 7 (Ravdin building, 7th floor). I received no orientation, no specialized training. On my first day I had a patient assignment and I took care of my patients. This is what HUP graduates did, that's why HUP nurses had a reputation for being the best.

Ravdin 7 was a 40-bed medical telemetry unit best known for treating patients with chronic recurrent v-tach referred from all over the country. Patients with chronic v-tach, or ventricular tachycardia, suffered sudden unexpected very rapid heart rates that were fatal unless converted immediately. They were a very unstable and unpredictable group, Ravdin 7 was definitely a high stress unit.

About a month after starting my new job I was working night shift. I had taken the elevator up to Ravdin 9 to borrow something and decided to take the stairs back down. I found a man laying face down on the steps. He was warm but was not breathing and had no pulse. I gently pulled him down the steps to the landing. I had to think fast, what did they teach me? I started CPR (cardiopulmonary rescusitation) and after several cycles I quickly jumped up, pushed open the heavy fire door, and shouted for help, call a code. I returned to my man and continued CPR for what seemed a lifetime, nobody was coming. I had made the decision not to move this man again because of a possible spinal injury from his fall plus I didn't think I could move him safely while trying to hold the heavy door open. Again I interrupted CPR to open the fire door and shouted for help. The code team was looking for me and finally took over. I told the code leader what I knew and what I did. He decided to continue rescusitation on the floor in the stairwell. I had made the right decision. There were enough people there now to hold the door open and work out of the crash cart.

This was my first of many codes I participated in throughout my nursing career but was definitely the most unusual. I felt it was initiation by fire. I was cool and confident and appropriately responsive on the outside but inside I was trembling. The surge of adrenaline rushed through me as I reflected on what had just happened—a man's existence teetered precociously between life and death and my actions made a difference.

I enrolled in the hospital's education benefit program and met with my academic adviser at Penn's School of Nursing to guide me through the requirements for my BSN. I had to take and pass "challenge" exams for every nursing course I had taken at HUP's program to get credit. They were not fun, they were equivalent to massive comprehensive final exams. I took every challenge exam they offered and passed each one. What I was lacking were the required electives outside the School of Nursing. I registered for two courses every fall, spring, and summer without fail. It took me four years to complete all the requirements and finally I received my Bachelor of Science in Nursing from the University of

Pennsylvania compliments of HUP. All I had to do was be determined, organize my time, work hard, and act on an incredible opportunity to further my education.

During the four years I worked at HUP I lived in downtown Philadelphia and learned to truly love this extraordinary city. I lived at 11th and Spruce for one year then moved to 24th and Chestnut where I lived for three years until I left Philadelphia. I loved this apartment just east of the Schuykill River, I was within walking distance to everything I loved plus HUP was an easy walk just across the river. I had season tickets to the symphony, played tennis, attended my classes, worked full time, and frequented the many, many diverse restaurants Philadelphia is known for. I ate my first cheese steak, bagel, calzone, and reuben sandwich. It was a great city.

I had interesting boyfriends too—a Philadelphia cop, a HUP doctor, an airline pilot, to mention a few. Each showed me more than I had known before but I eventually lost interest in each. Someone called me a heartbreaker. I just wasn't ready for a long term commitment.

I continued to learn, developed my management skills, and grew as a new nurse. I worked many night shifts because my classes typically met during the day or late afternoon. Working night shift on Ravdin 7 was by no means the type of job where you prop up your feet and snooze until morning. These people were sick. There were two long corridors with 20 patients each and two nurses. I took one side and the other nurse took the other side. Typically after report from the evening shift they would sit around and chit chat for some time before checking the patients. This always bothered me and I knew Miss Hartung would have a fit. So immediately after report I would announce I was making my "breathing" rounds. I took this very seriously, I was just entrusted with the lives of 20 people. I started at one end of the long corridor and quietly entered each room. If they were sleeping I watched their chests rise and fall with each respiration. If they were awake I introduced myself and determined what I could do for them. This was always my practice.

One night I made my same announcement and took off to check my patients. But this time one of my patients was not breathing. I called the code and started CPR immediately. Sandy's breathing rounds became standard practice.

During the four years I worked on Ravdin 7 I met so many incredible people. One was a nurse getting her masters degree at Penn's School of Nursing. Several days each week she spent time with us helping to fine tune our skills. She helped us write a patient education brochure for our patients with chronic recurrent v-tach and had it published. She later became an associate dean at the School of Nursing and past-president of the American Association of Critical-Care Nurses. Her name is Kathleen McCauley, a person who impacted and influenced my young nursing career.

One morning after I finished working my night shift I was walking home crossing the bridge over the Schuykill River. The bridge was lined with excited people on both sides, I asked what was going on. I was told this was the route the pope was using to go to his next engagement. So I waited with the others and soon the popemobile slowly approached where I was standing. Pope John Paul II waved and blessed all of us. This man glowed with God's presence. I was not Catholic but I respected his role as the world's moral leader.

I had been working on Ravdin 7 almost four years and I would complete my BSN in a few months. I was feeling restless and ready to do something different. I really had no ties to Philadelphia and I felt ready to move. But where? I talked to my sister Teresa and her husband Rick. He suggested I look into the Armed Forces, something I never would have considered but I liked the idea. I talked to recruiters with the Army and Air Force and decided I wanted to do this. I was 24, would enter as a First Lieutenant because of my nursing experience, and was guaranteed an assignment at Tripler Army Medical Center in Hawaii.

I made a weekend trip home to broach the idea of military service with Dad and Mom. I wasn't asking for permission or approval, I was discussing an important decision I had made and hoped they would support it. I think I completely shocked them when I told them I wanted to be an Army Nurse. Mom was upset and deferred to Dad, Dad asked lots of questions and just wanted to be sure I considered everything and the consequences. They didn't think the Army was for me, they were very concerned. My Pappy Lesher had been invited to join us for dinner and when I could talk to him alone I spoke to him about the Army. We talked, he asked questions, we talked some more, then he told me it was a good decision. A few short months later he died while mowing grass, a heart attack. He never saw me in my Army uniform, at least from earth's perspective. He was a great man in my eyes.

The next week I called my recruiter and told him "Let's do it. I'm ready." I met him at the Center City recruiting office where an Armor Lieutenant Colonel was expecting me. I raised my right hand and was commissioned as a First Lieutenant in the Army Nurse Corps.

Sandra Stuban, Army, Class-A uniform

Chapter 4
An Army Nurse

*"When you cannot make up your mind which of two
evenly balanced courses of action you should take—
choose the bolder."—W. J. Slim*

I was on my way to Hawaii and my first job with the
Army. The flight was long and as I closed my eyes, once
again, I considered my recent decisions. I had left a great
job at a great hospital in a great city with a great
apartment and great friends to do something quite
unconventional. Nevertheless, this was for me. What drew
me to the Army was the opportunity to see nursing
practiced outside my comfortable realm in Philadelphia,
the prospect of seeing and experiencing life in our great
country, and simply the challenge of something different.
I was willing to accept the risk. Moreover, on a more
sentimental note, I simply loved my country. My Army
contract was for four years so if it turned out to be a bad
decision I could easily tolerate anything for four years.

I remember thinking about what I had just been
through at the six-week Officer Basic Course at Fort Sam
Houston in San Antonio, Texas. We spent most of our
time in the classroom learning four years of college
ROTC Military Science courses crammed into six weeks.
I noticed the Army seemed to have its own lexicon and
loved acronyms. I learned about uniforms, rank structure,

army structure, saluting, fraternization, military justice, nurses as officers, nurses as leaders, and a gazillion other topics. We exercised every day as a class, the Army called it PT (physical training).

Army nurses are expected to always be prepared for war, disasters, and mass casualties and use our skills in the most austere environments. I knew little about this and wanted to know more. All my experience revolved around hospitals, unlimited supplies, and easily enforced infection control.

As a class we went to Camp Bullis, a remote field training site, set up tents, and began learning what nurses do in a less-than-ideal environment to care for the sick and injured. For the first time I fired a M-16 semi-automatic rifle and .45 pistol, triaged mass casualties, and applied the concepts of NBC (nuclear, biological, and chemical) warfare. I celebrated my 25th birthday in a tent with people I hardly knew in one way yet in another way we were already uniquely bonded. We toasted each other with a bottle of gin and limes someone had smuggled in. We were a band of nurses.

One of my classmates, also assigned to Tripler, asked if I would be interested in driving with her from San Antonio to Los Angeles then fly to Hawaii from there. At the completion of the course we took off. Our route to LA went to the Grand Canyon, Las Vegas, and the Hoover Dam with the last segment flying enroute to the Hawaiian islands. I was already seeing and experiencing life in a way I never dreamed possible just six short weeks ago.

As is customary, my sponsor met me at the airport and took me to the hospital to sign in. Within a few days I had an appointment to meet the Chief Nurse, she met all new incoming nurse officers and gave me my assignment. I would work on the medical telemetry unit. This opportunity impressed me, I never knew the Chief Nurse at HUP, let alone meet her.

Tripler Army Medical Center was a striking coral pink color located on Moanalua ridge on the island of Oahu. It was visible for miles. Once a 1000-bed hospital immediately after World War II, it now maintained just over 200 inpatient beds and provided health care for Army, Navy, Marine, and Air Force members and their families.

Gradually I began to understand the Army. The medical telemetry unit I was assigned to was smaller than what I was accustomed to with less seriously ill patients. Taking care of sick people was the same across our country, I deducted. But the Army did things differently in other ways that really impressed me.

First, the LPNs (Licensed Practical Nurses) were enlisted soldiers (91Cs) who were young, energetic, and eager for promotions. They were self-driven and respected the nurse officers. The LPNs I had worked with in Philadelphia were middle-aged women who walked slowly and did little without being told.

Second, I was introduced to the role of wardmaster. This senior enlisted soldier, usually a staff sergeant or sergeant first class, worked side by side with the head nurse. This relieved the head nurse of many responsibilities and allowed her to spend more time with her staff and patients if she desired. My head nurse at HUP never cared for patients and always seemed consumed with administrative requirements.

Third, the mood was different in a way that was difficult to describe. To call it camraderie or a "band of brothers" didn't seem adequate. People from other areas of the hospital sought me out, "Are you the new Lieutenant? Welcome." I did feel welcomed.

That's how I met Anne, another single first lieutenant nurse. She suggested we go to single's night held every Friday at the Officer's Club at Hickam Air Force Base to meet new people. So off we went. It was packed with hard bodies with mean haircuts. The band was fabulous, the dance floor gyrated with wall to wall sweaty couples. The atmosphere was casual and comfortable with everyone at ease with everyone else. We were all the same in one important way—we were all young single officers.

Something strange happened that night, my first night at this Officer's Club. I met someone who made my heart twinge and made my heart squeeze a little harder. I didn't know if I believed in love at first sight, but cupid's arrow hit both of us pretty hard. His name was Garry, a first lieutenant finance officer. What I saw that night was a six foot two inch confident man with a big smile who enjoyed being the life of the party. We talked and danced and talked and danced. Subsequently we spent every day together for the next eight weeks until he left Hawaii for his next assignment at his Advanced Course in Indianapolis. I learned he was a VMI (Virginia Military Institute) graduate, his Dad was a retired infantry colonel, and his maternal grandfather was a retired two star general. Feeling assured I was not spending so much time with some covert psychotic drug dealer, when he asked me to marry him, I said yes. Six months later we married at St John's Lutheran church outside Elizabethville, Pennsylvania.

Before making that decision, I lived in an apartment halfway up the mountain in the town of Aiea. The small lanai looked out over a golf course that offered an unobstructed view of Pearl Harbor. I could see the big ships and envisioned the devastation that happened here so many years ago on December 7th to this beautiful island and harbor. At times I simply couldn't believe I was here. My assignment had been shortened to one year so I could join my new husband-to-be. I worked, learned the island, learned the Army, went to the beach, played tennis, and thoroughly enjoyed everything this assignment offered. But something was missing. Somewhere during my nursing education at HUP or getting my BSN at Penn, I was smitten with the insatiable desire to always learn and always improve myself. I enrolled at the University of Hawaii and began work on my master's degree.

I left Tripler and Hawaii after just one year to join my new husband at Fort Hood, Texas. Although separated for nine months, during this time we managed to see each other several times and get married. We rented a small house in Copperas Cove not far from base. We were ready to start the business of being married together, finally.

I met the Chief Nurse at Darnall Army Community Hospital where I requested to be assigned to the Intensive Care Unit. He concurred. I had no formal critical care experience but I had an incredibly strong nursing education followed by four years of hands-on nursing experience at one of the best hospitals in the country. I wanted a clinical challenge and I was smart enough to learn it in short order. I was ready to learn something new and different.

Fort Hood was a huge Army post about 339 square miles located in the rolling hills of central Texas 60 miles north of Austin. Darnall Hospital supported all active duty soldiers and their families plus retirees living in the area. There were two critical care units—the Coronary Care Unit (CCU) was designated for those with severe heart problems and the Intensive Care Unit (ICU) took everything else. It was known as a fast paced, wild place to work. That's where I was assigned.

As with any ICU, all new employees had to learn the technology unique to the unit. I learned it all—pumps, monitors, special catheters, waveform interpretation, arterial lines, ventilators, and much more. I watched, asked questions, read, researched, and asked more questions. With my strong clinical background and my intense desire to be challenged, I taught myself to be the best.

I worked there almost four years, saw some pretty incredible things, and met some pretty courageous people who fought desperately for their lives. A young warrant officer shot himself in the mouth in a suicide attempt and lived. A young soldier suffered a traumatic amputation of his hand during a training exercise. A young wife riding as a passenger on a motorcycle was split up her middle from between her legs when the bike crashed. A soldier was run over by a tank during night training and survived because the muddy ground was forgiving but every bone from his waist down was shattered, his intestines were ruptured, and his bladder had burst.

A typical day was never typical simply because our patients were so unstable. On one day things seemed relatively quiet but in a matter of minutes two patients coded at the same time. A man with esophageal varices (like hemorrhoids) ruptured these fragile vessels and began vomiting frank blood and arrested. In the next room a young lady had a grand mal seizure and stopped breathing. This was the norm. Working here was not for everyone but it was definitely for me. I loved this fast paced, unpredictable environment.

On another "typical" day, I was next up for the next admission. After receiving report from the emergency room, I met my new patient—a big strapping strong first lieutenant in a terrible car accident. As each hour passed, his body started shutting down and his organs began to fail. The insult to this young healthy man was simply too massive. We managed to keep him alive until his parents arrived then we allowed him to die with dignity, his mother and father at his side. My head nurse and I were invited to attend his memorial at a chapel on base. We arrived wearing our Army white nurse's uniform, everyone in the packed chapel knew we were the ones who tried to save this young man's life. Incidents like these are tough on the heart. I knew first hand how fragile life was. One minute a promising young lieutenant had dreams, hopes, and aspirations, the next minute his life is snuffed out. I learned to value life a little more and respect death as a natural part of living.

There were so many other young men and women who touched my life who teetered between life and death, young people, like myself, who felt strong, indestructible, and on top of the world. Some lived, some died. I always cared for my patients passionately and professionally but in my own private sanctuary I cried and mourned when a young life was taken before its time.

I became a runner. Running was not only a great physical release but it also cleared my mind after working a tough shift. I would review and reflect and problem-solve in my mind's quiet refuge devoid of the chaos and frantic attempts to save young lives. Running helped me keep life in the proper perspective. And central Texas helped by offering many opportunities to participate in 10-kilometer fun runs.

I got to know my new husband too. I worked many night shifts and weekends but we managed to deepen our relationship. We were both serious about our work and supported each other. We ran together, made short trips together, and traveled to Austin frequently to experience this beautiful city and its fine restaurants. When he had two back surgeries in two years about one and a half years into our marital bliss, I was right there. I was his wife, nurse, and friend, I never felt inconvenienced or impeded on.

Patti Kinder was my best friend. She also worked in the ICU and had the same work ethic and values as I did. But as is customary in the military she was reassigned to another location too soon. I missed her terribly but the

Army allowed our paths to cross again at a later assignment.

My critical care skills matured and I constantly sought the challenge to always improve, I wanted to be the best. I took the ACLS (Advanced Cardiac Life Support) course, a difficult stressful combination of written exams and practical hands-on scenarios that tested appropriate responses to various serious cardiac events. I earned my certificate first time up and renewed every two years without fail. Failure rates were high.

When I had an opportunity to take the ATLS (Advanced Trauma Life Support) course, I jumped at it. None of the other nurses in the ICU were interested, they thought I was crazy. I traveled to San Antonio and learned about trauma care. The course was incredibly difficult, stressful, and intense. The final written exam was complex and intricate but the practical hands-on exam was even worse. I was given a scenario and a real moulaged patient. The instructors wrote down everything I said, everything I did. On that final day, those who passed the grueling standards received certificates. I received an honorable mention but no certificate. When I spoke to the cadre about what this meant, they looked at my written exam, a clear pass. They looked at my practical exam, no errors. Then they looked at my nurse caduceus on my uniform and said nurses cannot receive ATLS certification regardless how well they perform.

I was furious. I knew I couldn't change this injustice and fumed the whole drive back to Fort Hood. I knew I was better than many of the physicians in this course and I didn't need a certificate to prove it.

I loved working in the ICU, there was always something different to challenge my gray cells. I thrived on the unexpected, the fast pace, and the constant learning. But when I learned that an instructor position was advertised in the Nursing Education and Staff

Development offices, I applied. The nursing supervisor gave me the verdict—I was too good of an ICU nurse to move me from critical care. It was like being patted on the head and slapped on the face at the same time. After the ATLS outcome and now this, I had to figure out how to productively channel my disappointment, anger, and frustration. I didn't like being told no without a reasonable justification.

Through my running I had my "ah-hah" moment. When I had everything mentally in order, I presented my idea to my head nurse. She supported me 100 percent and I was off and running. I developed a 12-month education program for the ICU staff. The monthly presentation would be taught by the military nurses and be repeated several times each month so all ICU staff working other shifts could attend. The topics ranged from pulmonary assessment to gunshot wounds to total body failure. In addition I prepared and submitted each presentation for Continuing Education (CE) credits, an important requirement for most nurses to renew their license. Then I advertised the CE presentations each month hospital-wide using a snappy header on an eye-catching flyer. My education program was immensely successful, the presentations were always well attended by nurses throughout the hospital. From the time of inception until the first presentation was an incredibly short time, I was compulsive about making this happen.

Why did I do this while a staff nurse in an incredibly busy ICU? Part of it was I loved the teaching and learning aspect of my profession, another part was the challenge and hard work needed to make this worthwhile program perfect. But I had to admit that Dad's bullishness reared its head inside me, I had to prove to myself and maybe to others that even though I was denied a deserved ATLS certificate and denied the instructor position, the staff education program I developed was first class and far exceeded what was coming out of the Nursing Education office, all while working in the busiest unit in the hospital. And people noticed.

When I had worked enough critical care hours to qualify, I decided to take the CCRN certification exam. This certificate was the highest recognition for a critical care nurse and extremely difficult to earn. Well known for its low pass rate, I bought the prep book and started serious studying. I was concerned because the ICU did not do certain procedures so I had no clinical experience in these areas and I was sure the exam would cover it. I would have to apply the principles I worked with every day to those procedures I had no hands-on experience. I read every word in this book cover to cover then drove to Dallas and took the exam from hell. I left feeling mentally beat up and immediately started checking answers in my book. When I eventually received the letter with the results, I didn't want to open it. I didn't want to see my failure in an area of nursing I absolutely loved. But I passed! And first time at bat, I was ecstatic.

In one of my last months working in the ICU before my reassignment to Germany, I was working night shift. The configuration of the unit had ten rooms in a row with a long nurses station facing the length of the rooms, openings at either end to exit, and a large central monitoring system displaying each patient's vital numbers and waveforms in the middle. On this particular night, in the wee hours when all the patients were stable and the nurses finally sat down, about four or five of us leaned back in our chairs around the central monitors to catch our breath. Talking, but always keeping a watchful eye on the monitors, I saw one of the patient's regular heart rhythms spontaneously change to v-tach (ventricular tachycardia), a lethal rhythm if not converted immediately. Without a word I leaped over the nurses station, ran into the patient's room, and raised my fist. Before delivering the sternal thump, I raised my eyes to his bedside cardiac monitor and saw he had converted back to his normal rhythm on his own. With my fist still raised I looked back at the patient who looked back at me with eyes the size of saucers.

When I casually returned to my colleagues behind the nurses station, they were in hysterics, chuckling and snickering so intensely they had tears running down their faces. They had never seen someone move so fast, jump so high, and cause a patient to convert spontaneously just by looking at me. I laughed with them as they told the story over and over again, I admit it must have looked pretty funny. The story was passed on, embellished, and exaggerated while I became notorious in the process. It was on this note I left for my new assignment. I loved this ICU, I loved the terribly sick people I cared for, I loved the camaraderie and competence of my peers as we worked as a team to give our patients the absolute best care. We were good, simply the best. And I missed everyone.

Germany was the homeland of my ancestors, I knew Jonathan Lesher arrived in Philadelphia by boat from the Black Forest region in about 1748. I was eager to meet the country of my forefathers and start my three-year assignment. We flew into Munich where Garry was assigned, I was assigned to the military hospital in Augsburg about 50 miles to the west. After finding an apartment at the midway point in the small town of Esting, just a few miles from Dachau, I was ready to start work.

The hospital was small like most US military hospitals scattered across Europe. This hospital had everything needed to support the troops within a certain geographical area. Located in a building that was never intended to be a hospital, the Corps of Engineers was building a brand new hospital immediately beside the current structure.

I met the Chief Nurse and learned I would be the acting head nurse on a Medical-Surgical unit while the present head nurse attended a 16-week military course. I jumped right in. It was obvious I had a different style and approach than the current head nurse and when I saw things that made no sense, I asked questions and was told they always did it this way. Meeting with the Chief Nurse, I clarified as an acting head nurse was I maintaining the status quo or did I have free rein to make changes. He gave me the liberty and I never looked back. He didn't know me, yet, but in the next three years we did many good things for this hospital.

In the months that followed I established myself as a hands-on leader, I was out there where the work was done, advocating for my staff and patients, and making changes to make their work flow more smoothly. I managed by walking around and spent little time in my secluded office. The nursing staff knew I came to them with serious ICU experience and called on me frequently to draw blood, start IVs, and do arterial blood gases on difficult patients. I was always a high energy, positive person so when one of the senior surgeons, a colonel, approached me, he told me in his experience a unit takes on the personality of its head nurse and he thanked me. This was quite a compliment coming from the hospital's deputy commander.

The Chief Nurse moved me to the other Med-Surg unit as its permanent head nurse, the staff welcomed me with open arms. They already knew what I could do and I didn't disappoint them.

During my orientation to the military medical presence in Germany, I learned about the master's programs offered by Boston University specifically for military members assigned overseas. Main campus professors accepted assignments in Germany to teach their courses. With the Army's Tuition Assistance program paying 80 percent of costs, this was an opportunity I couldn't pass up. So I enrolled in their Master of Education program majoring in human resource education. I planned my classes carefully so I would complete all requirements for graduation before my three-year assignment ended, which I did. Graduation activities were held in Heidelburg and included a chartered boat cruise celebration down the Rhine River. Commencement was special too with German Chancellor Helmut Kohl as keynote speaker, a large man who towered over Boston University's president Dr John Silber who introduced him. In the end I left with a Master of Education from Boston University and all I had to do was work hard.

Because the military hospitals across Europe were small, a cadre of ACLS (Advanced Cardiac Life Support) instructors traveled to these hospitals to teach and test the course. I don't exactly know how this happened but I was invited to attend the instructor's course and join this elite group. My personnel record showed I was certified in ACLS, attended ATLS, CCRN certified, and had four years clinical experience in a busy ICU and they wanted a nurse on their team. I was their choice. So through helping to teach this important course I traveled throughout Germany.

The Chief Nurse called me to his office, he wanted to improve the pass rate of the ACLS course at our hospital which he believed was due to unfamiliarity with reading EKGs (electrocardiograms) quickly and accurately in stressful situations. Of course I could help. I developed a full day EKG interpretation course that I taught twice a year prior to the ACLS course. My classes were always well attended with nurses, LPNs, doctors, and dentists. The end result showed an incredible improvement in

ACLS certifications with better responses to cardiac emergencies.

My plate was always full, that's the way I liked it. I never felt harried or out of control, everything was carefully planned and organized. So even though I was a head nurse and teaching ACLS and teaching my EKG course and attending classes with Boston University, I was always looking for new and different opportunities. It came.

All the Army hospitals across Germany were ordered to provide a certain number of medical professionals to form a team to medically support a six-week training exercise in Turkey. As far as I was concerned this was what Army nursing was all about, always being ready. Of course this was a period of peace so training was imperative. I volunteered and the Chief Nurse supported me.

The team met in Ramstein and flew by cargo plane to a remote field landing site somewhere in western Turkey. From here our team and mobile hospital were transported by Chinook helicopters to the place we would set up our hospital. On this barren landscape on the edge of a goat herder's path, the "campus" of our hospital took form—emergency tent, operating room tent, Med-Surg tents, pharmacy, lab, dental tent, and more. I was assigned emergency and worked 12-hour shifts seven days a week. We saw few casualties but the practice and training were invaluable.

We had two large sleeping tents, we were either sleeping or working, one for the boys and one for the girls. Once the cooking unit was set up we had hot meals for breakfast and dinner. And eventually we had a shower unit. This may sound ridiculous but we were medical professionals and were expected to be clean—the field version of infection control. In all my training I had never encountered a field shower and it was quite a unique experience.

Lady's shower days were Monday and Thursday, gentleman's Tuesday and Friday. A small ante-tent allowed enough room to get naked, the connecting large tent had about 20 or more shower nozzles protruding from the sides. There was one person to a nozzle and enough room to get organized. The shower sergeant called out "Ladies, the water comes on in one minute... three, two, one." You better be ready because the water came just like that and no temperature control. There was two minutes of water. "Ladies, the water goes off in 30 seconds... three, two, one." This was one minute of frantic scrub time. "Ladies, the water comes on in 30 seconds... three, two, one." This last two minutes of water had to take care of all the remaining soap. And when the shower sergeant counted down the final turn off, he must have chuckled when he always heard our moans and pleas for a little more water. He always ignored us, what power he had.

It didn't take us long to master this biweekly ritual and eventually we incorporated shaving our armpits and legs and washing our underwear. Even though we lived next to a goat herd, we didn't have to smell like one. We were still ladies.

This training was so important, in the event of war we always had to be ready to support the troops. That was what Army nurses did. Six-weeks later we were back in our world of eight-hour days, flush toilets, and 20-minute showers. We were better nurses because of it.

A passion of both my husband and I was our interest in traveling. We were best friends and made each trip a wonderful experience. I was enthralled with the centuries and centuries of history throughout Europe and beyond and the diverse cultures that were so different than my own. I learned that Augsburg was a city founded more than 2,000 years ago and that Martin Luther, the founder of the Lutheran faith, lived here in the 16th century. I think my Germanic genes were invigorated with the culture—the food, the beer, the fests, the architecture, the organization and orderliness of the people. I loved it all.

Luckily these were years of relative peace with no concerns of insurgencies, suicide bombers, or terrorism. Travel was safe and we traveled extensively. Our first major trip was to Egypt and over the next three years we traveled to France, Italy, Rome, Belgium, Czechoslovakia, Greece, Israel, Kenya, and Russia. Every trip was special in its own way, I was enlightened and more informed than ever before about the world I live.

Again the Chief Nurse called me to his office with a vision he wanted to realize. He wanted to create a program for good but overweight soldiers in the combat arms units to help them lose weight. He gave me his abstractions and asked if I could make it happen. He knew I could and I did. It was a huge project in addition to everything else I was involved with but I loved the challenge of transforming an idea into a concrete and successful service. I called it the FLEX (Fat Loss and Exercise) program. The main tenets of the intense three-week program included dietary instructions, an exercise regime, a support group, and weekly weigh-ins. I managed all the logistics of marketing, staffing, communication with the soldiers' units, and a graduation ceremony. A new group of eight overweight soldiers was admitted every month. FLEX was such an extremely successful program that a waiting list had to be established and I frequently took calls from company commanders urging enrollment of one of their soldiers. The Chief Nurse had another feather to put in his cap.

I was busy and happy with everything I was doing so I was completely shocked when I came home from work one day to find Garry waiting for me with packed suitcases. He wanted a divorce. There was no forewarning, no prior discussion, and denied another woman. He gave no explanations except he didn't want to be married any more. Without going into painful details I didn't understand, I grieved and grieved and saw a chaplain counselor and grieved more. I felt I lost my best friend. This wasn't my idea of the commitment taken with marriage but I also had no power or persuasion to change what was happening to me. Six months later the divorce was final and just like that I was single once more after seven years of marriage. I never saw him again.

The pain struck to the core and scarred my heart that slowly eased with time but never completely disappeared. I dealt with this personal trauma by completely immersing myself in my work, my many projects, and my master's degree with Boston. I moved one mile from the hospital and took a long weekend trip to London with my nursing friends.

With about five months left to my assignment in Germany the Chief Nurse called me to his office to discuss my next move. He recommended me for a job as a nurse counselor with either recruiting or ROTC and showed me a list of about five locations where positions would be open that summer. For nurses these jobs were highly sought and considered extremely career enhancing. As a single officer I chose the ROTC nurse counselor position at Omaha, Nebraska. I asked to leave as soon as possible.

The city of Omaha exuded with classic midwest charm and charisma. My office was with the ROTC military science staff at Creighton University but my Chief Nurse was located at Fort Lewis in Washington state. So I flew there to learn what this job was all about. During this period there was a tremendous interest and mission for commissioning nurses through ROTC. I was essentially a hands-on consultant for my geographical area of responsibility that included the five states of Nebraska, Iowa, Minnesota, and North and South Dakota.

During my orientation I must have met a gazillion people, all interested in meeting the new nurse who could help them recruit nurses. While observing the ROTC cadets at their summer camp at Fort Lewis I met one more person. Steve Stuban introduced himself and said he knew me from a previous assignment. I said I don't think so and continued walking. When he started rattling off names of mutual acquaintances he had my attention. He had been the project engineer overseeing the construction of the new military hospital in Augsburg and remembered seeing me during a walk-through in my white uniform surrounded by my staff. OK. I kept walking.

Back in Omaha I realized the enormity of my job and the independence I was given to do whatever needed to be done. It was obvious this job was not for the meek, lazy, or conventional thinker. I punched no clock, made my own schedule, and knew my success, or failure, would be measured in numbers. Nursing numbers. Failure was never a part of my fabric. So after reading, thinking, considering, analyzing, and fact-finding, I took off like my hair was on fire. I had to work until the work was done.

After contacting every ROTC department with a nursing school I learned they all wanted my help desperately and immediately. These combat arms officers were expected to increase their nurse numbers but they lacked the knowledge and confidence to make it happen. They lacked what I called "nursespeak." I educated each designated recruiting officer about nursing in general and Army nursing in specifics. They listened when I spoke with the dean at their School of Nursing. They learned when I spoke to classes of nursing students. They eventually could speak about nursing with ease, honesty, and enthusiasm plus I was always available for the tough questions.

I thoroughly enjoyed promoting my profession. When speaking to classes of nursing students I believed I was particularly effective because I was able to compare the four years I worked at one of the most prestigious hospitals in the country, the Hospital of the University of Pennsylvania, with my experiences in the Army. I didn't mince words and never came close to imitating Goldie Hawn's perceptions in Private Benjamin. I was a straight shooter, direct and sincere. There were always many questions and I always made myself available for the many private questions. These questions not only covered Army nursing but also women in the Army. I realized I was the first female officer many had ever seen. I was not only representing Army nursing but was also an ambassador for women in military service.

Captain Steve Stuban was the recruiting officer at the University of Iowa, one of my schools. He was persistent in getting to know me and I would have to say that our first few "dates" were phone dates, each lasting many hours. When he broached the idea of coming to see me in Omaha, a four-hour drive from Iowa City, I was hesitant. Though I met him briefly at Fort Lewis, I honestly couldn't remember what he looked like. I had met so many people there plus I wasn't looking for romance after being recently divorced. But he was extremely persuasive and I eventually succumbed.

When I opened my door that day, I saw a man about my height (I am 5'7") wearing rayban sunglasses and a backpack. Steve was charming, funny, and intelligent. He seemed to have values, a work ethic, and drive similar to my own. Over time I learned he was a West Point graduate and a first generation American of parents immigrated from the Ukraine and Germany. We enjoyed each others company and eventually worked out a system of seeing each other every other weekend alternating the four-hour drive between the two of us.

By the end of my first year in Cadet Command, more and more nurses had entered the ROTC programs in all my schools. All the recruiting officers and their professors of military science knew me well and knew I was always there to support all their nursing efforts and activities. I received the most incredible annual evaluation from my Chief Nurse and the Commanding General of Cadet Command's 4th region. And because of restructuring of these regions, three more states were added to my area of responsibility—Colorado, Wyoming, and Montana. My second year was even busier than my first.

I thoroughly enjoyed what I was doing, I loved educating my fellow officers and nursing students about nursing and being a female officer. Because of my work ethic and the ingrained principal that you work until the work is done, I may have seemed ubiquitous. I never gave excuses. My job was to support my colleagues which I did in a way they had never experienced before and I gave them credit for every new nurse who entered their programs. My aggregate nurse numbers spoke for themselves.

My courtship with Steve was not always smooth. When my sister Teresa invited me to join her family for a week at Disneyworld, I jumped and asked Steve to join me and he agreed. But as this time came closer I realized I was not comfortable with the implied seriousness of our relationship. I told Steve I didn't want him to go with me, sold his plane ticket, and several days later received an envelope by mail with my house key inside, postmarked Iowa City. Later we continued seeing each other.

At another time he brought up the topic of marriage, not a proposal but a discussion. I said no, no, no, no, no. I was not comfortable here. I had been proposed to several times in my life and had been seriously burned by the one

I accepted. At the age of 33, I knew Cupid had no magic arrows and love was a state of mind not a palpitation of the heart. I was fiercely independent, a man was good to keep my bed warm on cold nights. At least at this point.

My work consumed my days, I was promoted to major, and Steve persisted. When I began considering my next career move after my two-year assignment as a ROTC nurse counselor, I was uncertain. My relationship with Steve had matured and I began to wonder about our future together. During a weeklong vacation to the Jersey shore with my parents and sisters, Steve asked Dad's consent to marry me. When he did ask me to marry him later that day and produced a ring, I said yes.

We were married in May 1991 at West Point. Steve wore his dress blue uniform and I wore a beautiful white trained gown with my major's rank pinned to the traditional garter on my left thigh. It was a beautiful wedding.

The next challenge was planning our next move together. After considering many options, we moved to Kansas City, Kansas where Steve attended the Command and General Staff College at Fort Leavenworth and I attended the University of Kansas for an advanced degree after being accepted for the Nurse Corps' two-year fully funded graduate program.

My academic adviser Dr Roma Lee Taunton was a woman I would never forget. Her soft southern drawl was no indication of her tough professional standards. Combining her direct approach, research focus, and meticulous attention to every detail, she was clearly a leader and remarkable scholar. When she told me about the newly approved joint degree program for a Master of Science in nursing administration and a Master in Health Services Administration I said I wanted to do it. She looked at me with skepticism, told me it was designed as a full time three-year program, and asked if I was collecting master's degrees. This woman could be intimidating but I calmly said "No Ma'am, just knowledge." She didn't know me, yet. Here I had an opportunity to complete two masters degrees, learn the business side of health care, and all I had to do was work hard. It seemed like a no-brainer, at least to me.

My course load was incredibly heavy and she helped me plan my courses carefully so I would complete all requirements in the two years the Army gave me. I was the first person enrolled in this new joint degree program, she didn't want me to fail. But failure was not an option. So when I volunteered to help in the undergraduate skills lab one semester, she pointedly asked why I was doing that. Another semester I volunteered to help with research day, she asked me the same question. Throughout my two-year stint there I also served as graduate representative to the Student Nurses Association with one of my classmates. I think Dr Taunton eventually figured me out. I was organized, thorough, and actively pursued a challenge. Oh it was tough, especially the health care finance, economics, and law. But when I finished with an overall grade point average of 3.9 Dr Taunton was proud. I was invited to join the International Honor Society of Nurses, Sigma Theta Tau, and was inducted at a lavish dinner with KU's faculty and other student inductees. This was quite an honor.

In my final semester I met an Air Force nurse in one of my classes. Ruth Anderson and I seemed to have so much in common, her infectious laugh simply made you join in. We both had Dr Taunton as an advisor and later learned that she enjoyed advising military nurses because of our discipline. Little did I know that I would see Ruth again at a future assignment and again after both of us retired from military service.

Sometimes the Army is so unpredictable. Steve and I negotiated for our next assignment together and offered to go to Fort Riley, also in Kansas. But the Army said no, no, no, we must go to Hawaii. I had started my military career there and unknown at this time I would end it there.

I would be remiss if I didn't include this escapade that seemed to define the relationship Steve and I had. At this point we were married for two years. We had decided to drive our two cars east to ship them to Hawaii from the Baltimore port and visit with Dad and Mom in Pennsylvania for a few days. We borrowed walkie talkies (this was before cell phones) and planned to follow each other for the drive from Kansas to Pennsylvania. At the first gas stop, while Steve was paying at the counter, I entered the small convenience store to use the bathroom. He turned to me and without saying a word did this circular thing with his finger—let's go or make it fast or speed it up. A minute later I came out and he was gone. He wasn't at the counter, he wasn't in the small store. His car was gone. I looked everywhere. I was infuriated. Why would he leave without me? It made no sense. All I could rationalize was that he was in such a hurry that he left and expected me to catch up. So I got in my car and tried the walkie talkies, no response. So I took off and entered the interstate but after a few minutes I pulled off the road and waited 15 minutes. I tried the walkie talkies constantly with no response. I just couldn't understand why he left without me. I went through every possible scenario in my mind but nothing made sense. So I drove, with a seething anger, toward Pennsylvania, by myself. When I stopped at a motel for the night in West Virginia, I called home to tell Dad and Mom I would be there the next morning. Dad answered on the half ring and said Steve had been calling every 30 minutes, everyone was waiting for my call to know where I was. I hadn't known if Steve was in front or behind me but I learned he was behind me. And at that first gas stop way back in Missouri, Steve had moved his car behind the small store where I couldn't see it. I still don't understand why he moved it there. To this day if someone does the circle thing with a finger I go crazy. I guess we were two independent minded individuals who were not in synch with each other.

So I returned to Hawaii after a 12-year hiatus, it was quite a difference going as a senior major as opposed to a lieutenant. When I met the Chief Nurse I learned I was being assigned as the Head Nurse of the OB-GYN Clinic. My mouth dropped, I wasn't an OB-GYN nurse. It was like telling a civil engineer to work as an electrical engineer or an estate lawyer to work as a trial attorney. I was assured they needed someone with strong administrative skills rather than clinical skills. What could I say? So I geared up for my next challenge.

I did my homework and it didn't ease my concerns. It was the busiest military clinic on the island with 6,000 to 7,000 clinic visits each month. A medical staff of eight physicians provided oversight and instruction to the approximately 20 residents in this OB-GYN residency program. The clinic was huge with four long corridors of exam rooms and the waiting room was equally large and impersonal.

After figuring out how things worked and meeting all the nursing personnel who supported this immense operation, I scheduled an appointment with the department Chief. Colonel (Dr) Eric Salminen was a model officer and leader, easily approachable, and had the build of a runner, which he was. I quickly developed a deep genuine respect for him. At this first meeting I could not envision the special professional relationship that would develop and the breadth of his confidence in me as I presented plan after plan to improve his clinic. He truly became my champion. But at this initial meeting I ask for financial support to attend a five-day OB-GYN clinical nursing conference in Cinncinati, Ohio. He approved it. I absorbed everything like a sponge, I had to. And after five days I had the knowledge, coupled with my past clinical experience and common sense, to begin to feel comfortable in my new role.

The other RN and I saw every newly pregnant woman in their first trimester, we were their first appointment where we discussed such important topics as smoking, alcohol use, breastfeeding and so much more. At first glance it would seem like no big deal but in reality we saw approximately 50 women every week. And when the big ships and aircraft carriers returned to port at Pearl Harbor, the numbers were even greater. This was a very fertile island.

The clinic had enough going on to keep anyone crazy busy. But the status quo was never satisfying to me when I could see potential improvements to make things even better. I was a nurse with a business degree, I saw things with a slightly different perspective.

The huge waiting room was filled with what looked like '60's era chairs arranged row after row like a movie theater. The chairs' vinyl was cracked and torn and many were repaired with duct tape. I found the whole scene disgusting and couldn't imagine the impression this made with our customers. This waiting area accommodated as many as 50 to 100 women at any given time. I asked Colonel Salminen if the department had money to implement the plan I described to him. This was his first leap of faith with me, I didn't disappoint him. The end result was incredible—contemporary chairs arranged in small groupings, large plants, and a completely different ambiance.

Education had always been a high priority for me, especially patient education. My predecessors must have felt this importance too because there were a gazillion pamphlets and brochures on just about every female health issue imaginable in the clinic. However they were completely inaccessible to the women who should have them, tucked away in drawers in the bowels of the clinic. I knew other clinics simply filled their waiting room walls with pamphlet holders but that certainly wouldn't work in this clinic. Imagine a woman taking health information about herpes or genital warts in full view of 50 to 100 eyes. When I had my plan finalized and had Colonel Salminen's support, I implemented my version of a mini patient library in the waiting room. Using room partitions to create a private enclave, an education center was born that not only respected a woman's right to privacy but was aesthetically pleasing. I was pleased to see how many women used it as they waited for their appointment but I also saw the residents use it to give information to their patients. I showed my nursing supervisor the new education creation and the next day she returned with the Chief Nurse. The need for education was apparent, the solution was novel, inexpensive, and effective.

It was time to address another issue that had gnawed at me since day one. With every bone in my body on high sensitivity, I again approached Colonel Salminen with a problem and my solution. When the residents called their patients from the waiting room, they called them by only their last name "Smith." I told him ladies don't like that, the residents should call them Mrs. Smith or Ms. Smith or sergeant Smith or Pam Smith but never just Smith. He could have thought I was crazy but it was the fine-tuning at this point that could change public impressions of the clinic from good to better to great. Colonel Salminen mandated the change immediately and I saw the change the next day.

I always looked beyond the busyness where it was easy to be consumed with the sheer volume of women who entered our doors every day, every month. Again considering the opportunity to educate I formulated my plan and again presented my idea to Colonel Salminen. Knowing the clinic saw about 7,000 women monthly that equated to 21,000 women quarterly. I proposed starting a quarterly newsletter called Women's Health available to all women entering our clinic. I envisioned the newsletter to have four recurring features—a short article with an OB focus, another article with a GYN focus, clinic improvements, and a resident profile. This became a huge success and the clinic became known more and more as a place that truly cared about women. Every quarter I left a new newsletter on Colonel Salminen's desk for his review, changes, and approval. And by the end of the day it was returned to me, he never made any changes and he always approved enthusiastically.

Like everywhere I ever worked, my plate was always full but completely organized and planned. So in addition to my daily work of seeing the OB ladies, being a telephone advise nurse, responding to phone consults, managing and evaluating my nursing staff, preparing for the upcoming JCAHO (Joint Commission on Accreditation of Healthcare Organizations) inspection, and responding to crises that inevitably arose, I looked at the bigger picture and a better way to do things. I was known as a forward thinker who could make things happen.

Less than a year in the clinic, I received a call after clinic hours to report to the Chief Nurse's office. I was told the Lieutenant Colonel promotion list had just been released and I was selected below zone, meaning I was selected early. So with just 14 years of military service I would be promoted before my peers. Obviously I was ecstatic and thrilled that my hard work had not gone unnoticed over the years.

Though the clinic kept me busy, it wasn't my whole life. Hawaii was a beautiful place to live. I was probably in my best physical shape in my life, working out and running at least five days a week. It was at this point that I told Steve if we were going to have children it was now or never. Unfortunately the clock was ticking, I was 38 years young.

Of course I was smart about the importance of the preconception period and since I knew I would be pregnant in the near future I stopped the wine with dinner, stopped drinking coffee, stopped adding salt to my food, and started taking Folic Acid. Some may have thought this was compulsive, I saw it as being smart. So when I got pregnant, I knew it immediately, I expected it. Because of my age I was classified as "advanced maternal age," a term I understood but loathed its application to me. I could run circles around most women 20 years my junior. My pregnancy was completely uneventful, I continued running then walking, and my weight was perfectly managed. I felt every growth, every change, every kick. I was enthralled with the idea of a life growing inside me. Every night in the quiet before sleep comes, I listened to my body and felt my baby talk to me through his movement. I already loved him so much. So when my water broke at 4 a.m. at 32 weeks, eight weeks early, I was completely baffled.

My doctors presented me with an unusual proposition— stay hospitalized on bedrest, eat and feed this baby inside me, and try to get to 34 weeks when the lungs mature. That's exactly what I did. Somehow something inside me must have known that time was up because my labor started exactly on time, exactly 34 weeks. Being my first pregnancy I expected a long labor but I called Steve anyway. Boy was I wrong. After six hours and two pushes, Nicholas Lesher Stuban came into this world yelling. I had gone through my entire labor alone and Steve and my doctor almost missed the big exit. They both arrived less than five minutes before this beautiful baby boy was born. When I finished all my duties, I got up, went to the bathroom, and walked to the NICU (Neonatal Intensive Care Unit) to reunite with my new son. I never had an epidural, never had any analgesic. I viewed childbirth as a completely natural event, I didn't understand what all the commotion was about.

All 5 pounds 2 ounces of Nick's tiny body were perfect, he was breathing without any problems which was everyone's biggest concern. Like all newborns, he lost weight initially and when I took him home a week later he weighed 4 pounds 13 ounces. I loved this little boy that I had grown inside me more than I could ever imagine. He was constantly hungry, after all he was accustomed to continuous nutrition in his warm and wet sanctuary. Technically he should still be there six more weeks but he couldn't wait. So I fed him every time he was hungry, which was at least every two hours, with the liquid gold that only a mother can make. At night early on, Nick developed a pattern of kicking his crib mattress when he was hungry, and of course I heard his every sound. In the dark with no dramatics, I nursed him before a cry ever left his mouth. Interestingly one morning Steve made the comment I must feel rested since I was able to sleep through the night. The truth was I had been up three times to feed Nick, he never knew.

When I was on bedrest in the hospital, the Chief Nurse visited and left me with an interesting proposition to consider. After my six-week maternity leave she wanted me to leave the clinic to assume a newly created position as the hospital's Patient Education Coordinator to prepare for the upcoming JCAHO inspection. Steve and I discussed this tempting offer and considered all the pros and cons. Ultimately he advised me it was too risky to take the job, if the inspection went poorly my career would be tainted. I did consider his points but that wasn't me. I craved for the challenge. I wasn't afraid of hard work. Again, in my mind, failure was not an option. I saw this as an opportunity and I was never one to let opportunity pass me by. I accepted the job.

Nick was six-weeks old when I was promoted to Lieutenant Colonel. I had easily lost my pregnant pounds except five pounds I carried in my milk-laden breasts. To my dismay, when I tried on my Class A uniform that always fit me to a T, I couldn't close my jacket over my breasts, not even close. Quickly Nick and I visited a tailor to see what could be done and with their expertise solved my problem. Military men certainly never had this dilemma to deal with.

The promotion was like none I had ever had. The auditorium was filled with more than 100 friends, colleagues, OB-GYN doctors, Dad and Mom, Nick, and Steve. I was so touched by everyone's support and the many many traditional leis they adorned me with. I wished Nick was old enough to remember this important day with me.

I started my new job with relatively little guidance except to meet JCAHO's standards that included new emphasis on patient education. Actually I was pleased with this arrangement, I could exercise my independent thoughts, think outside the box, and create and guide new innovations. I was starting from scratch on everything from my own job description and hospital regulation on patient education to more grandiose visions of seamless horizontal and vertical consistency of patient instructions.

Fortunately, I was assigned an assistant to help me bring all my ideas and plans to fruition. Joe Washington, a retired sergeant and ex-wardmaster, was my right hand man who was equally passionate and devoted to creating a new patient education infrastructure and presence at Tripler. We were a team.

At one of the Patient Education meetings I chaired, one of the physicians, actually the Chief of Medicine, told me about a fully functioning patient education library that had to be relocated due to the BRAC (Base Realignment and Closure) decision to close Fitzsimons Army Medical

Center in Denver. He thought it had been unofficially "promised" to another Army hospital on the mainland. I knew I had to move fast.

Establishing a patient education center was always on my agenda but I expected to grow it slowly from nothing. Acquiring one fully loaded was beyond my expectations. This was big, an opportunity of unbelievable proportion. After making a gazillion calls, discerning support, identifying potential space, and much much more, I briefed the Commanding General about my intent with a letter of justification in hand. He signed it immediately and the plan was set into motion. In an incredibly short time I was notified that our request was approved and the library was being boxed and shipped immediately. Then began the task of converting dusty boxes of books into a functioning library. And so in short order Tripler had a stand up, fully functioning Patient Education Center. Phew, what a whirlwind. I loved it.

Of course when JCAHO arrived, the inspectors lauded our patient education programs. I was thrilled. But there was still much more to do.

Nick was such a big part of my life. I was so fortunate that Tripler had a day care center called the Keiki Co-op in one of the hospital's outlying wings. What this meant was that we traveled to and from work together and when I had late work to finish he could come to my office. But most important, I could continue breastfeeding. When he was ready to eat, his caregiver paged me with a code we established, and I went there and nursed my growing baby. I could not have asked for a better arrangement.

My patient education initiatives continued growing and expanding, there was so much to do. I loved identifying problems, creating solutions, and making them happen on a large scale, at the hospital level. I absolutely loved what I was doing.

One day I was called to the Chief Nurse's office. She had nominated me to serve as special assistant to the Chief of the Army Nurse Corps, a general officer, in Washington, DC. I couldn't even begin to describe the emotions of being selected for such a prestigious assignment.

My life was full and satisfying. I had a beautiful baby, I was promoted to Lieutenant Colonel early, I had a job in patient education I loved, and I was selected to serve with our Corps Chief. I felt on top of the world, indestructible, and on the path to many more successes. Nothing could stop me. Nothing.

Sandra and Steve Stuban, wedding, 1991, West Point, New York

Sandra and Steve Stuban, 1994, in Dress uniform, the Engineer Ball, Hawaii, one year before Sandra's diagnosis of ALS

Sandra and infant Nick jog together at their home in Kapolei, Hawaii.

Chapter 5
The Diagnosis

"You have to accept whatever comes, and the only important thing is that you meet it with courage and with the best that you have to give."—Eleanor Roosevelt

When Nick joined our family he added a dimension to my life that was previously absent. I was mature with an established career when this little baby captured my heart. I took him everywhere with me, he quickly became a part of everything I did. So when I returned to running shortly after he was born, of course I took him with me. I bought a baby-jogger from one of my friends and we were off and running. Even though I hadn't run for many months while I was pregnant, the transition back was not difficult. I was still in great shape.

I also had to start preparing for my first post-baby APFT. The Army Physical Fitness Test was done every six months and consisted of doing as many pushups as possible in two minutes, as many situps as possible in two minutes, and running two miles as fast as possible. Throughout my military career the running and pushups were relatively painless but the situps were always an effort. So when I began practicing my situps in preparation and could not do one, I was surprised but thought it was due to my pregnancy. Maybe the stretched abdominal muscles needed more time to recover even though I was never terribly large and delivered six weeks early. I kept practicing.

But after many weeks, I still could not do one situp. I guess I was more puzzled than anything else. I couldn't imagine my pregnancy had seriously damaged my abdominal muscles but I really didn't know. I called a physical therapist I knew and told her my concern. She saw me, examined my abdomen, gave me an exercise regime, and said to come back in three weeks. I practiced religiously but made no progress, I was becoming frustrated. I was no wimp.

When I returned to physical therapy for my follow-up appointment, my friend had no explanation for my problem. She called the physical medicine physician to examine me but he had no explanation either. He scheduled me for an EMG (electromyelogram) the next week. I was anxious to get to the bottom of this mystery.

The EMG was quite an experience. Small needles were inserted into a muscle, electricity was fed into the needle, then the muscle response was measured as a waveform on the nearby oscilloscope. I closed my eyes and went somewhere else in my mind as the needles and electricity entered different muscles one by one. The doctor never said a word as he methodically checked different muscle groups. With the printout in hand he stepped out of the small treatment room for a short time. When he returned I saw the concern on his face, I asked if he found something. He wasn't sure and wanted to test more muscles. So I endured more of the same, testing different muscles. When he finally finished, we talked. He noticed I had fasciculations, or muscle tics, all over my body. That plus the waveforms from the EMG were consistent with ALS.

This was the first time I heard the word ALS. I was 38 with a three month old baby. This doctor took the time to talk to me about ALS reinforcing that this was by no means a definite diagnosis. He sent a consult to neurology, the experts, to further evaluate what was going on. I was strong and healthy, I knew he had to be wrong but at the same time a fear was planted inside me.

I told Steve everything about this visit and its outcome. He had the same opinion I did, that he was obviously wrong. I was physically fit and always took care of myself. I never smoked, never took elicit drugs, and kept my body tuned with regular exercise. So we went about our lives as usual with little concern that anything major would be discovered.

Colonel (Dr) W, the chief of neurology, took my consult and became the medical sleuth investigating and hoping to rule out ALS. My first impression was he seemed to be informed about ALS. At my first meeting with him after answering extensive questions, he did the usual subjective muscle strength tests, checked my reflexes, and observed my many fasciculations as part of my history and physical exam. At this point the only physical sign I had that something was wrong was my inability to do situps and the new finding of muscle twitches. He outlined and explained all the tests he ordered. I understood there was not one test to make a final diagnosis but rather it was made by ruling out a host of other nasty diseases and watching the progression of symptoms. I was to hope that one of these other tests would be positive, anything was better than ALS.

As I started this trek through the battery of tests I was being subjected to, I researched each one as I continued my readings of anything related to ALS. I didn't like what I read about ALS at all. In the beginning I vaguely knew about ALS from nursing school but I never cared for anyone with it. I knew people with polio and cared for a lady with myasthenia gravis in the ICU at Fort Hood but ALS was a completely different animal.

The first test was a blood analysis for lyme disease, it was negative. The 24-hour urine collection for the heavy metals of lead and mercury was negative. As I lay on the table entering the tunnel of the MRI (magnetic resonance image) getting images of my head and cervical spine, I thought how ridiculous it seemed that I should be hoping it showed something "positive" like multiple sclerosis, cervical strictures, or a brain tumor. Everyone told me again and again, anything was better than ALS. This test was also negative.

During my consult with the endocrinologist, he discussed some uncommon causes of neurological symptoms and ordered a blood test for thyroid and parathyroid levels and a bone density evaluation for proper utilization of calcium. All were negative.

During the many weeks of tests, I started noticing very subtle changes. I was never one to take elevators and I could easily bound up four flights of steps without breaking a sweat or breathing hard. All of a sudden this became difficult. The other change I saw was I was having difficulty getting up from a chair. Nobody noticed these slight changes but me. Fear started creeping into my thoughts.

When all the test results were available, I met with my neurologist Colonel W again. Considering the EMG, the other negative test results, the fasciculations, changes in my reflexes, and the slight changes I recently experienced, he made the diagnosis of ALS. He told me about a new drug, riluzole, just approved by the Food and Drug Administration for ALS that extended a person's life by two to three months. I said, excuse me, you must mean two to three years. No, it's months. This was the first and only medication known to slow the progression of ALS. But in my eyes its claim to extend life by just a couple months seemed ridiculous. He continued saying he could special order the drug and I could start taking it immediately. Wait a minute, I said, I can't take this drug. I was breastfeeding my baby plus I planned to have another baby. He looked at me like I was from outer space, didn't I know this disease will kill me in two to three years? But I was firm in my decision to wait and I would tell him when I was ready to start the drug.

Then Colonel W told me he was ordering another blood test to be sent to a special lab on the mainland to evaluate my DNA to determine whether I had sporadic or familial ALS. I knew 90 to 95 percent of people with ALS had the sporadic type, the other 5 to 10 percent had a mutant gene that could be inherited and passed on generation to generation. Scary stuff. When the results eventually came back I learned I had the sporadic type. For me that meant ALS was not passed to me from Dad and Mom and I could not pass it on to Nick. With all the bad news I was hearing lately this was a respite of relief.

Finally Colonel W told me I should get out of the Army now, take my baby home, and spend time with him until I die. He could initiate the paperwork to make that happen immediately. Now I looked at him like he was from outer space. My whole life I worked, enjoyed working, and wanted my baby to understand the Lesher work ethic. I had no intention of taking the easy out. With the few minor symptoms I felt I simply told him I wasn't ready to medically retire from military service, I would tell him when I was ready.

I also told Colonel W that I could not yet fully accept the ALS diagnosis based on the evidence so far and wanted a second opinion. He agreed, wrote the consult, and arranged for me to see a neurologist in downtown Honolulu. This physician was my age, kindly, and seemed thorough but hesitant. So when I asked him how many people with ALS he had seen, I wasn't surprised by his answer. None. Of course I asked Colonel W why he sent me for a second opinion to a physician who had never seen ALS. I wanted a second opinion, he said I had one. Then I wanted a third opinion, he said he couldn't support that.

About this same time, I received a call from the personnel office to sign the packet prepared by Colonel W to be sent to the Medical Review Board in the mainland for my separation from military service. I was aghast. He initiated this without my knowledge or consent. I spoke to the personnel officer about the situation, my desire to stay on active duty as long as possible, and my options. On his recommendation I wrote a rebuttal to the president of the medical board that was included in the packet and off it went. Weeks later the result was returned in my favor, my rebuttal had been strong and convincing enough for me to continue my work on active duty. But when Colonel W was informed of the result he was irate. He hadn't known I submitted the rebuttal and was furious that I had the gall to do such a thing and then be successful. At this point I lost my respect for this man who was so set on following his own agenda that he forgot his patient, me.

My desire for a second, or third, opinion was not lost. I did my research and learned I could get another medical opinion especially since an ALS diagnosis was career ending and life ending. I worked with the personnel office and told them I wanted to be evaluated at an ALS center where they knew ALS. I received approval and orders to fly to San Francisco to be seen at the ALS Research Center at California Pacific Medical Center. The personnel office contacted Colonel W to complete the required paperwork and of course he growled and complained but there was nothing he could do except comply. I had initiated and arranged all the logistics to get another opinion about a lethal diagnosis that I was absolutely authorized to receive. Why would he deny me this? I would deal with him when I returned from the mainland.

I flew to San Francisco alone enroute to a weeklong military senior leadership conference in San Antonio, Texas I had been scheduled to attend. I arrived at the ALS Center with my heart pounding with anticipation. All I could show them were my fasciculations, vague weaknesses, and peculiar waveforms on an EMG. As I opened the door to the clinic, I encountered a woman about my age and build. She walked with a cautious, unsteady gait. I couldn't help thinking to myself I was strong enough to never let myself get to that point. But I was still in the mindset of being physically tough, indestructible, and in control.

The waiting room was small with pictures of Lou Gehrig adorning the walls. I was the only person there and I wondered about that but I later learned all the activity took place inside the clinic itself. When I was taken to a small exam room I met Dr Robert Miller, a world-renowned ALS researcher. He and one of his fellows were expecting me and knew everything about my ALS work-up. They were warm, informative, and thorough. I didn't have to ask how many people they had seen with ALS. They asked expected and unexpected questions, had me do situps and pushups, watched me get up from the floor, and did another EMG among many other things.

This EMG was different though. They only tested the great muscle below my thumb and were looking for a neurological condition that mimics ALS but treatable. It was negative as all my other tests had been. I spent many hours there and was hoping for a definitive answer to the ALS question before I left. But even with all their expertise a quick ALS diagnosis was impossible. A muscle biopsy could be added to the arsenal of tests already done, but more importantly the progression of symptoms was the only true gauge.

I left feeling unsettled. Everything supported ALS even though I showed minimal weakness, even though my main complaint was I couldn't do situps. I didn't like the idea of passively waiting for ALS to completely envelope my body and life. I still had many things I wanted to do but I was becoming more and more concerned.

My first order of business when I returned home to Hawaii was to address my issues with Colonel W. After considering the best approach I decided to write a factual, pointed missive of my complaints. I wanted every issue to be heard in its entirety. Besides forcing his own personal values on me of how I should live my life by suggesting I go home and die with my son, and unilaterally submitting the paperwork for my separation from the Army without my knowledge or permission, he denied my request for another medical opinion though it was authorized. I had worked with people and patients my whole life and believed and practiced the concepts of mutual respect and self-determination. His approach with me was unacceptable and he needed to know it regardless of his position and rank. He was not my advocate or had my best interests in mind. My decision to address these issues had nothing to do with being given a bad diagnosis. Rather it was completely based on what I considered disrespectful and insolent treatment. I wanted to remove him as my neurologist and have someone else assume and manage my care.

Of course he responded, in writing, to each issue and defended himself on all counts. My intent was to alert him to his poor judgements and hopefully change his approach and attitude toward future patients. My care was transferred to one of his staff neurologists, Major (Dr) C. Unfortunately he proved to be a mere puppet of his boss with the same arrogance and indifference to his patient's preferences.

Even with all the test results and subjective subtle changes and expert opinions, I was still conflicted about a definitive ALS diagnosis. I wasn't ready to have a tentative death sentence change my plans or my life. So when Nick was six months old, I stopped breastfeeding and actively pursued getting pregnant to give Nick a brother or sister. Each month I didn't conceive I felt ALS's presence more strongly, I was frightened. After three months I stopped trying and regretfully accepted that Nick would be our only child. What convinced me was the increasing difficulty taking stairs, more difficulty getting up from a chair, and now beginning problems just walking. But I still hated the idea that ALS was beginning to dictate my life.

The muscle biopsy was the last outstanding procedure. And even though my weaknesses were mounting, I still felt compelled to have this final invasive biopsy done. Under conscious sedation in the same-day surgery suite, a muscle sample was taken deep within my upper thigh and sent to the Armed Forces Institute of Pathology in Maryland. When the results returned many weeks later reporting muscle changes consistent with ALS I was devastated. I had tried to prepare myself for this eventual conclusion but it was virtually impossible to accept I could die in two or three years. I was too young and too healthy, I had my career and my family. I simply had too many things I wanted to do.

I received and finally accepted the undisputed ALS diagnosis around Thanksgiving. All hope for another less destructive cause was now gone. The holidays passed while I tried to get a grasp of my life, or what was left of it, and considered what this meant for my husband of four years and my new baby.

ALS had already forced my decision about having more children. Now it forced my hand again. I hated the thought that ALS was now ruling my life and my decisions. The next two things I knew I had to do were so painful it was almost unbearable. First I had to turn down the opportunity to work with the Nurse Corps general officer in Washington, DC. I knew it was the beginning of the end of the military nursing career I loved. Then, even more heart wrenching, I had to tell Dad and Mom their daughter had a disease that could kill me in just a few years.

Lessons Learned

* Be your own advocate.

Stand up for yourself with passion. Nobody knows your strengths, personality, and degree of determination better than you do. Only you know what is truly in your best interest. This simply means taking charge of your life, your preferences, and your desires especially in the face of something as uncontrollable as a life-changing diagnosis or event. Pursue those things that make sense, are important to you, and are priorities in your life.

* Do your research.

At the first mention of ALS, suddenly I couldn't learn enough about it. This is imperative in any situation that threatens to consume your lifestyle and your thoughts. Knowledge is powerful. Not only does it allow you to have intelligent, interactive discussions with your physician, but it also provides you with the ammunition to make informed, practical choices at a time of adversity and great uncertainty.

* Make your own decisions.

In the months leading up to my diagnosis, I made many decisions my physician disagreed with, such as waiting to start riluzole, seeking another opinion at an ALS research center, and choosing to stay on active duty as long as possible. He wanted to make these decisions for me without considering "me." In hindsight, all my decisions were the right ones. For me. Just as when a physician gives you a prognosis of two years to live, you shouldn't passively accept this prediction. I decided to forge ahead on an unknown path with little guidance. It's a decision only I could make. And it was again the right one.

•   Tell your parents (family) early.

I chose to wait until my diagnosis was certain before I told Dad and Mom. I should have told them earlier. My rationale was I didn't want to unnecessarily alarm them since I was in the middle of the Pacific and they were on the east coast. But by waiting I caused hurt, disappointment, and more concern with the closest members of my family who only wanted to support me. I should have told them at the first mention of ALS.

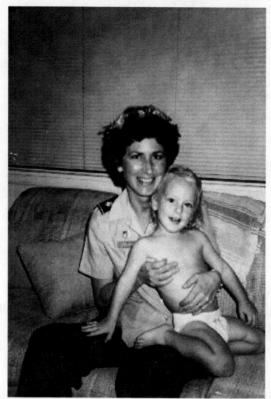

Sandra with one-year-old Nick, just learning to walk; Sandra beginning to have trouble walking

Chapter 6
The Slow Decline

"When one door closes, another opens. But we often look so regretfully upon the closed door that we don't see the one that has opened for us."—Alexander Graham Bell

These were the most uncertain years of my life. I had so many questions I knew had no answers. Being the proactive person I always was, I really had no idea how to prepare, physically or mentally, for impending total paralysis. I still couldn't imagine this would happen to me. It was a major source of frustration, but it was coming whether I liked it or not, whether I was ready or not.

Shortly after the definitive diagnosis I knew I needed help adjusting to the prospect of becoming a quadriplegic followed by an untimely, unwanted early death. After all I was essentially a newlywed with a new baby, I had responsibilities to Steve and Nick. As the hospital's patient education coordinator, I knew what programs were available and who their point of contact was so I reviewed the list for anything that might help me, even abstractly. I considered the death and dying seminar that was offered quarterly but quickly ruled it out as being a bit overkill.

Then I noticed a support group for young people with cancer facilitated by a co-worker from my first assignment in Hawaii 14 years earlier. I didn't have cancer but I certainly had many of the same concerns and fears and maybe even a shorter life span than some with a cancer diagnosis. As I thought about this I envisioned sitting among the group as a staff visitor yet at the same time garnering critical information that could save my faltering emotional health. And after even more thought, I called Joan Foley RN, the group facilitator. This was a huge step for me, my first real independent act against ALS. When I started asking about the group, Joan immediately asked who the patient was. I paused for very long moments, I really didn't know what to say, I hadn't prepared for this. When I said it was me, she said "Come see me right now." It wasn't a question, she was firm and meant it.

As I walked to the other side of the hospital to Joan's office in radiation oncology I wondered what I had done. Nobody knew I had ALS except my neurologist, the chief nurse, Steve, and I. I hadn't even been able to tell my closest friends yet. And here I was going to talk to a nurse I worked with a long time ago. The ball was already in motion, I followed it through. Joan was waiting for me and as her door closed, all I could do was cry uncontrollably. It certainly wasn't what I had planned but then ALS was never in my plan.

What happened over the next hour and then weekly for the next year changed my life. Joan was, and is, an incredible woman. And all who know her recognize her smile, laugh, and genuine care and concern for others. I experienced it first hand from a situation I never thought I would be in. There was so much she taught me that I still use today. In addition to encouraging me to read books for guidance and inspiration, she stressed one particular maxim that I used over and over again in the next years to help me accept the many losses ALS would force upon me—when you lose an ability, you must grieve the loss as you would grieve the death of a friend, then move on. I was just beginning to lose my first ability.

I began falling. The strong body I was accustomed to started to slowly fail me. My first fall was devastating emotionally and terribly frightening because it was so unexpected. As I had done hundreds of times before, I lifted Nick from his high chair after his meal. But this time my legs crumbled beneath me. I held him tight and as I hit the floor he stayed on my chest. Nobody was hurt and Nick actually laughed thinking it was a new fun adventure but I had to start grieving my "friends," my physical abilities I would lose.

Then I began falling at work, but only twice. I became super cautious and learned to make adjustments to the way I normally conducted business. I could no longer trust my legs, my strong runner's legs. The first time was going up some steps with some friends. The second time I was walking down a long corridor. In both incidences my legs simply gave out with no warning. I was beginning to understand how I would slowly become paralyzed and it frightened me. I chaired several important hospital committees and now scheduled these meetings as close to my office as possible to minimize my walking and the likelihood I would fall in a public place in uniform. The many other informal meetings I had were now held in my office instead of traveling throughout the sprawling hospital complex. And Joe, my assistant, became my legs more and more.

Despite these "inconveniences," there was nothing about my job I couldn't do and I continued my innovations with the same gusto. When we had the new patient education center ready for operation adjacent to the hospital's public library, I planned and advertised its grand opening and ribbon cutting with the hospital commanding general as guest speaker. Interestingly I saw Colonel W, my neurologist, in the crowd as I led the ceremony though we exchanged no words. According to his timeline, I would be out of the Army sitting at home waiting to die. No thanks. I had things to do.

More weaknesses that were more significant kept happening and as they did I dealt with them, they all had solutions. I developed foot drop and had to lift my legs high to walk or I would trip on my toes. So physical therapy designed AFOs (ankle foot orthotics) for me. They were simply plastic braces held in place with Velcro and kept my feet straight instead of allowing them to drop when I walked. I wore them under my uniform pants to hide them and my ALS diagnosis.

When I could no longer rise from a seat at normal height, Joe found a way to raise my office chair. When my wrists went to same way as my ankles, I used wrist supports to use my computer. When I could no longer lift the receiver of my phone, I used the speakerphone exclusively. For every gradual loss there was still a resolution available to keep me completely functional. Joan helped me tremendously through these initial failures of my body and I grieved the loss of each "friend." I was still totally independent and needed help from no one, which of course I preferred.

Soon other failures became more significant and more scary. I knew it was time to start the process for my separation from the Army though I hated the thought. But I was no longer the fit military officer I once was, I couldn't even give or return a salute any more. I couldn't raise my arm and hand to my brow. I told my new neurologist I was ready to start the ALS drug riluzole and I was ready to resubmit my packet to the medical board that would end my military service. This was very important because their decision would determine how much medical support I could receive later through the VA (Veterans Affairs) health care system. And I knew I would need a lot.

It's difficult to describe how I lived with such absurd changes to my life, lifestyle, and livelihood. It was almost like being emotionally numb during the day and at night, with only myself, I grieved. Although my friends supported me greatly, I felt alone with the madness of slow paralysis. But I didn't dwell on my losses. I grieved them like Joan taught me then moved on. I had a son to raise and he needed to know me as the person I always was, not some depressed, pessimistic thug. That wasn't me, never was.

The weaknesses continued and became more significant so now I had to start to rely on others to do key functions. When I no longer felt safe driving, Steve and I carpooled to work which was really no inconvenience since Tripler was just two miles from Fort Shafter where he worked. When I could no longer open the Velcro tabs to change Nick's diapers, Steve did it. When I could no longer do the laundry, Steve did it. When I could no longer write checks to pay the household bills, Steve did it. When I could no longer clean the house, I hired someone. In one way I felt bad that Steve had to assume more home responsibilities that were always mine yet a more equitable distribution of these tasks also seemed appropriate for two full time military officers with demanding jobs. I continued to prepare our meals as always. And I continued to spend important time with Nick.

Kids like to play on the floor and that's where Nick and I spent many hours. Even when I couldn't get up from the floor by myself I refused to ask for help. As distasteful and demeaning as it was, I crawled to the nearby stairs and slid my butt up step by step until I was high enough to stand up. It worked for me. And I insisted on reading to Nick, a lot. He sat on my lap and always listened intently. Soon it was his "job" to hold the book because I couldn't. He was about 18 months old.

The results of the medical board gave me a 100 percent service-connected disability and the paperwork was automatically sent to the VA office in Honolulu for processing and enrollment into their system. I started the process of leaving the Army, I would medically retire at the rank of Lieutenant Colonel after just 16 years of service and two years after my life-changing diagnosis. There is no doubt what I could have achieved in my military nursing career had ALS not interfered with my life. It was another goal unfulfilled, another loss to be grieved.

My very good friend Patti Kinder and Joe planned a retirement dinner and program for me at Tripler's officers club. The room was filled with about 60 friends and colleagues, nurses and doctors, pharmacists and administrators. I knew it would be an emotional evening and had tried to prepare myself for everything. But it was real tough when the evening began with laying a beautiful traditional Hawaiian flower tiara, or haku, on my head. But there were physical challenges that night as well. I couldn't walk up the two steps into the room reserved for our function. With Steve on one side and Patti on the other, they gave me the physical support I needed. Then I couldn't cut my meat during the meal because the utensil was too heavy. The waitress removed my plate to the kitchen and returned it with everything in order. I couldn't lift my tall glass of ice tea and asked for a high straw so I could drink by simply leaning forward. And finally when it was my time to speak, I couldn't stand. The microphone was moved to me so I could address my friends while seated. I had prepared my remarks in advance and every time I reviewed them at home I ended up with tears on my cheek. I was determined to deliver my speech with no tears, which I did, but there were many other wet eyes that night. Retiring at this point in my career was never in my plan but I was already firmly in ALS's grasp and they all knew it.

Steve was still on active duty and we coordinated his next move to the Washington, DC area to coincide with my retirement date. But there was much planning to be done anticipating the things I could no longer help with when I had always played a major role. Through the Army I obtained a collapsible wheelchair expecting that I wouldn't be able to walk the long distances in the airports. I tried to foresee any possible issues in the coming months before our move from Hawaii, I wanted no surprises, I wanted to be a burden on no one.

I knew I wanted to be involved in a clinical trial looking for answers to ALS's mysteries and knew through my online research that Johns Hopkins University in Baltimore had open enrollment to test a new drug made by Sanofi. I called them from Hawaii, explained my situation, and asked them to reserve me a place. They did just that.

When the time came to do my final out-processing for separation from the Army, it was tough, both physically and emotionally. Steve had to physically help me and I knew my dependence on him would only increase with time. There was much walking involved, steps into different buildings, and signatures required on a gazillion documents, all of which I had great difficulty doing. I couldn't have done it without him. But I was also emotionally drained. I was no longer a top notch, fit, fast charging, high energy Army officer and nurse. Who was I? I started to have doubts of the image I portrayed and how I saw myself. My future was so uncertain and I hated it.

The actual travel from Hawaii to National Airport in Virginia was interesting to say the least. This wasn't a leisure trip where you pack for a week, it was a move, something military folks everywhere understand. But this time I couldn't assist in the way I was accustomed to plus we had a two and a half year old, high-spirited toddler. I couldn't help carry the many large heavy suitcases or the various carry-ons, bags, diaper bag, stroller, car seat, and wheelchair. It seemed nuts. But Steve took it all calmly in stride and seemed to accept the challenge. Nick was your typical toddler, everything was an adventure that needed to be explored. Luckily, once we were on the plane, when we made a cocoon for him under the seat in front of us, he crawled into it and eventually slept most of the trip to the other side of the world.

I had tried to prepare Dad and Mom what to expect when meeting us at the airport, they hadn't seen us for about a year. Physically I really looked unchanged, only my muscles were failing, atrophying, and becoming smaller. I arrived in a wheelchair and it broke my heart to have them see me this way. But even though they had tears in their eyes, they were there for me and supported me 110 percent as always. And this never wavered in the tough years ahead.

The plan was Nick and I would stay with Dad and Mom while Steve stayed with his sister and family in Bethesda, Maryland to begin his new job and look for a house for all of us. If I was up to par I would have been actively involved in all this. If, if, if. I had to start thinking differently, I was not the same person physically though my mind still thrived on high energy and total involvement. My body could no longer respond to all my mind's desires. But to Dad and Mom I was the same as always. Of course we talked and of course they were sad but their outlook was we go forward from here. I never felt pity from them only total support and another set of minds helping me solve the issues that continued to arise with my gradual loss of muscle strength and function.

During my stay with Dad and Mom, I scheduled my first appointment at Johns Hopkins to enroll in their ALS clinical trial. I met Dr Jeffrey Rothstein, another world-renowned ALS researcher, but he was such a young and charming man to be involved with such a disgusting disease. Thankfully someone like him devoted his talents and intelligence to unlocking the mysteries that totally confounded the scientific community. I was accepted, enrolled, and began my initial monthly visits. The trial had three arms—one group received a normal dose of the drug, a second group received a higher dose of the same drug, and a third group received a placebo. My fate was decided by myself by randomly selecting a number, the pill's identify was unknown to both me and the research staff throughout the trial. At every visit I completed lengthy questionnaires, had muscle strength tests done, and did a respiratory vital capacity. At the completion of the trial 18 months later, I continued taking the mystery pill while analysis of the data began. And some time later I received a letter stating the results of this research. There was no significant difference in the progression of ALS between those taking the drug at either dose and those taking the placebo. Very simply, it failed. It was like a broken record, the same result reported over and over again in every other clinical trial ever done to attempt to control or conquer ALS. Oh, and by the way, my mystery pill was the regular dose of the drug. Not that it mattered in the least, it was just as effective as a placebo against my nemesis.

Between working and making occasional weekend trips to Elizabethville, Steve managed to find a house that met our specifications, primarily a home with all living accommodations on one level knowing I would soon be needing a wheelchair full time. I hurt inside thinking that again ALS was dictating our decisions but in my heart and mind I knew I had to be realistic and proactive about what the future held for me as much as I hated the prospect. So when we replaced the existing carpet we chose a wheelchair-friendly, low pile berber. When we saw an indoor scooter during one of our walk-throughs we bought it with the house. Anticipating my near future needs like this was very painful, I still couldn't envision myself in such a weakened state even though I began using a wheeled walker while staying with Dad and Mom. The simple act of walking became a dangerous major chore.

The next dilemma was that Nick couldn't stay with me alone when we finally moved into our house the fall of 1997. He was a very active two and a half year old, I could no longer change his diapers, and it just wasn't safe. As much as I wanted him with me I arranged for him to go to a daycare center where Steve dropped him off in the morning going to work and picked him up coming home. I was home alone all day with my growing paralysis.

Yet my mind still belonged to the body I'd always known. I had lost my immediate circle of friends and their close support when I moved from Hawaii. I had just moved to a new location, something I had done many times before with the Army, but this time I had no means to meet new people, to make new friends. I couldn't walk, I didn't go to work, I went nowhere. I felt trapped. Then I wondered what new people I met would think of me. Would they see me as an invalid to be pitied or the person I always was but never knew? Strong willed, competent, high energy, efficient. I had to resolve this conflict myself.

I needed Nick home with me so after much internal deliberation and with Steve's input, I placed an ad in the Washington Post for a nanny/home assistant, in reality I not only needed help with Nick, I needed help too. Steve and I interviewed and hired Maria who ended up staying with me more than five years until my personal care became too complex. She had no medical background other than CPR training. She worked full time Monday through Friday and was a godsend. She did everything I would do if I could.

I knew my breathing was becoming affected which was very scary. At night I was waking up frequently feeling like I needed to catch my breath. I needed to get my medical care established but my VA paperwork was lost somewhere between Honolulu and Washington, DC so I wasn't yet eligible to receive care at a VA hospital. I scheduled my first neurology appointment at Walter Reed Army Medical Center. The neurologist sent a consult to pulmonology where I was scheduled for a sleep study immediately when the pulmonologist saw that my breathing vital capacity was greatly diminished. He suspected sleep apnea where I would forget to breathe when I slept causing me to wake up gasping.

I arrived in the late evening to the sleep study lab and was greeted by a very courteous and competent technician who explained everything as she "wired" me up. As I remember she measured brain waves for REM sleep, oxygen saturation, breathing rate, leg movement, and probably more. When it was lights out I fell asleep instantly. Halfway through the night the technician was so disturbed by what she saw that she placed a BiPap mask on my face and told me to go back to sleep. That morning she explained everything. She said I probably had not been getting adequate REM sleep for about six months or more. On this particular night I stopped breathing repeatedly causing my oxygen saturation to drop then I would unconsciously wake up enough to breathe. This cycle happened over and over again. I never had any REM sleep until she started the BiPap then I immediately went into a deep REM sleep the rest of the night. She said she had never seen such a dramatic response. And so began my long-term relationship with my buddy BiPap.

I had never worked with a BiPap in my professional career but I knew it was a growing area of interest in the

ALS community. Bilevel Positive Airway Pressure, or BiPap, was a noninvasive form of breathing support that was used to assist the weakening muscles needed for normal breathing and to prevent the need for early intubation and tracheostomy. I began using my BiPap only at night with a small nasal mask but needed help with its proper placement because my fingers were no longer nimble or strong enough to appropriately adjust the straps to get a tight seal so Steve did it every night. The BiPap worked by giving me a breath when I forgot and for the first time in a long time I was getting restful, uninterrupted sleep.

Soon after my appointment at Walter Reed I received a call from someone from Paralyzed Veterans of America (PVA). I had never heard of this organization before but they certainly had an impact on my life in ways I never could have imagined. I learned they are strong advocates for military veterans paralyzed by spinal disease or injury. But when she offered to help locate my lost VA application, I said I would think about it. I was used to fighting my own battles. Over the next few days I did think about it and I really had no idea how to find my paperwork, so when she called back I said "Go for it." When she located my packet, she also expedited it through the review process, and I started receiving my monthly VA disability check shortly thereafter. Who knows how long I would have waited without her help. But she didn't stop there. After reviewing my paperwork, she said I was eligible for an additional benefit called the Aid and Attendance Allowance because of the paralyzing effects of ALS and my increasing need for assistance. This added money was to be used to privately hire someone to help me. I never heard of this benefit but it certainly would help pay for Maria's full time employment. This process took longer but she kept pushing for me and calling me to keep me informed.

When it was finally approved at the higher level, her work with me was done. Her name was Tammy Latteral and when I finally met her by chance many years later, I was astounded to see that she was in a wheelchair, it was her friend and means for independence. I never forgot her. She was a true and genuine advocate for me.

Because of Tammy's help, I could now register with a VA hospital to receive all my care. This began my long-term relationship with the Washington, DC VA Medical Center. I was initially concerned about getting my care through the VA but I quickly learned it was a state-of-the-art facility with caring, competent, and compassionate people. They were surprisingly responsive to my many changing needs. When I really needed a specialty mattress to prevent pressure sores while I slept, they provided the best, a dynamic airflow mattress. When I asked for a backup wheelchair, they suggested a motorized version. When we decided to renovate our master bathroom to include a roll-in shower, they helped subsidize the cost through a special grant program. We received the same assistance when we installed a platform elevator and acquired a wheelchair accessible van. Without the VA's assistance these purchases would have been very difficult. With them my life was decidedly more comfortable. I never expected this level of support and I appreciated it.

Everything I did became progressively more difficult to do. I tried with all my might, to the point of breaking out in a sweat, to do the simplest things but it was impossible. My muscles just wouldn't respond. Walking became impossible, so I used the scooter. I couldn't lift my arms to brush my teeth or eat, so I propped my elbows on the table or counter and leaned my head forward. I hated asking for help but Maria saw me struggling and always assisted. I didn't refuse because I was usually exhausted by this time. Through all this Steve helped me in the evenings and weekends when Maria wasn't with me. I tried to minimize what I needed but the truth was I needed help getting up from a chair, getting to the toilet, changing my clothes, getting into bed, and putting on the BiPap. It's difficult to describe how I accepted these crazy changes to my normally strong body. At times it didn't seem like my body, or my life, at all, it must certainly belong to a stranger. My mind still operated the tough, responsive body I always knew that was slowly failing me. But I continued to grieve each loss and I continued to try to move forward with my life.

When my sister Teresa invited us to join their family for a week at Disneyworld in Florida, I desperately wanted to go with Nick but I had to figure out the logistics and support I needed. After discussing the level of assistance I would require with both Steve and Teresa, we decided to go for it. I thought I would never have another opportunity to do this with Nick, he was three and a half. So with me in a wheelchair, the BiPap in a carry-on, and a very active growing boy, Steve got us all safely to Disneyworld and back. The hotel and park were so accessible and I was pleasantly surprised by their sensitivity to my inabilities. But it still didn't negate the extra measures Steve and Teresa had to take to accommodate me and the things I simply could no longer do. Despite this the week was a big success. My heart warmed seeing Nick have the time of his life and romp with his two cousins for a full seven days. It was a trip well worth the effort, at least from my perspective.

The VA continued its incredible support with my ever-changing needs as ALS slowly enveloped my body. They sent a nurse to my home to evaluate my situation and I met Joan Trelease, a retired Navy nurse, for the first time. Joan had the personality of a typical military nurse and we hit it off immediately. She told me about a special VA program called HBPC, or Home Based Primary Care, where I would be assigned a primary care physician, nurse practitioner, social worker, dietitian, and dental hygienist who would see me in my home. The concept was exciting and I enthusiastically expressed my interest in being a part of this program. Joan submitted my name and information for consideration and shortly thereafter I was enrolled. Joan became my HBPC nurse and made monthly visits. I quickly learned she was genuinely caring, clinically superb, and a true advocate plus she became my friend.

When I saw an advertisement in a disability magazine about an automatic page turning machine, I was intrigued. I had never heard of nor seen such a device. I had always loved reading but with my previous busy work schedule there never seemed enough time. Now I had time but I couldn't hold a book nor turn its pages. When Maria worked, she propped up my book and turned every page. In addition she would stop at the local public library every couple weeks and get and return books for me on her way home. The page turning machine was expensive so with hesitation I asked the VA if they could help. Well, it was an unusual request and they didn't have a contract with this vendor but I persisted. They eventually purchased it for me and when it arrived it was a godsend. I was able to turn pages independently using a sip-and-puff mouthpiece since my arms and fingers had become useless. It turned out to be one of the most important purchases the VA ever made for me.

Some time later I was contacted by a speech pathologist at the VA about an alternative means of communication, she suggested a computer with a special software program. As we talked and she explained the possibilities, I began to understand how far technology had advanced for those with disabilities. Without using my hands I could completely operate a computer, something I hadn't been able to do for many years. When the equipment arrived a company rep came to set everything up and teach me how to use the system. It consisted of a laptop with an EzKeys software program installed and a voice synthesizer attached. Then there was the infrared motion sensor that would detect my movement to operate the computer. When we evaluated different physical placements on my body that could reliably move, the best choice, even at this point, seemed to be my face, specifically my cheek. I learned the techniques easily enough but I lacked motivation, was uninterested, and was beginning to lose my enthusiasm for most things. I rarely used this important tool that later would become incorporated in my fabric. But for now other things I could not control began dragging me down so low it almost destroyed me.

The next three years became the darkest, most distressing times I ever experienced. My breathing became more of an effort forcing me to use the BiPap more and more until I was using it 24/7. I was totally dependent on it. My ability to walk ceased altogether and when I could no longer even stand with locked knees, I had to be lifted from one chair to another. I could no longer feed myself so when Maria was off, Nick would feed me. He was about four when he started sitting with me with a spoon or fork in his tiny hand and placing food in my mouth so I could eat, something I had done for him not many years before. Soon even swallowing became treacherous causing me to very carefully chew and swallow each mouthful. But despite my cautious efforts I was nothing compared to ALS's strength. Many times when I choked and food entered my trachea instead of my esophagus so I couldn't breathe, Maria responded quickly by doing the Heimlich maneuver. It happened so frequently that I began to loathe eating and of course lost weight. But the biggest insult to my psych was the first time I had to ask Maria to wipe my butt. All muscle movement slowly faded and with it the dynamic personality and inner strength I once had. But through all this I still tried to practice what Joan taught me in Hawaii, I grieved each loss though it was getting tougher and tougher. My grief was so intense I sometimes cried for days.

But something else also happened during this time. In addition to having few local friends for support and rebuffing computer access, Steve stepped back. The calm, resilient man I knew became angry and wanted to minimize the time he spent on my care. He realistically knew he couldn't work full time and provide for all my needs AND have time for himself. In a way I took responsibility, after all who gets married in the prime of life and expects something like ALS to steal his wife's livelihood just four years later. I had my own issues dealing with the insults to my body, but I also understood a spouse had his own separate stressors to contend with. My flitting feelings of apathy, uselessness, lack of motivation, indifference, worthlessness, and futility intensified and seemed to be reinforced. This had never been me, my personality never knew these words but somehow I lost my spark. I was trapped in a downward spiral of negativity I couldn't escape. I felt alone with this horrible disease, I was totally in its clutches and I was letting it devour me piece by piece, ability by ability. I lost my fighting spirit.

Early one morning with Maria, I began having more and more difficulty breathing with the BiPap. Steve hadn't left for work yet and responded to her calls for help. I couldn't breathe. I told him to get the ambu bag to force air into my lungs but I was still in great distress. Finally I said "Call 911." It was October 31, 2001, the day I would have died.

———————

Lessons Learned

- Seek emotional help immediately.

One of the most important decisions I made early on was to get emotional support from my friend and counselor Joan Foley. Granted, I had an advantage by being a nurse in a large medical center and knowing where to go, but the key is that I actively, independently sought the help I knew I needed. Her help and advice were absolutely indispensable. I strongly recommend finding an appropriate professional counselor to set you on the right path when you are hit with devastating life-changing news.

- Be creative to solve physical limitations.

As physical changes occur, there is usually a solution to resolve each setback. Sometimes the solutions are practical and straightforward, but sometimes it means thinking outside the box. Early on while still working, I moved meeting sites, used wrist supports, and relied on a speakerphone. It's important to keep tackling the obstacles rather than giving up in frustration and desperation.

- Enroll in clinical trials and research studies.

Since I was diagnosed with ALS, I have enrolled in one drug clinical trial and several research studies looking for trends, environmental causative factors, and genetic mutations. Though I realize I may not receive direct benefits from any of them, I feel I am making a contribution to science and society in my own small way. Participating in research is a personal decision but one I have personally found rewarding and satisfying.

- Accept help from professional organizations.

The help I received from PVA (Paralyzed Veterans of America) was immeasurable. I shutter to think I almost refused their help. Being new to the world of military disability, I knew nothing about the processes and benefits to which I was entitled. PVA was the expert. Other organizations have similar commitments and dedication. Don't be afraid to tap into their expertise.

• Learn about the technology available that benefits the disabled.

I was so ignorant of what technology existed for the disabled that I didn't even know where to look or who to ask. At this stage, almost by accident, I learned about computer access by means other than hands and keyboards and about automatic page turning machines. As I became more assertive and proactive later, I learned much more about available technology on ALS message boards, chat rooms, websites, magazines, and online support groups.

• Know that your spouse is not superhuman.

When you're caught up with your own trials, it's easy to forget the trials your spouse is dealing with. Juggling work, caring for me, father responsibilities, home maintenance, and personal time can easily take more hours than there are in a day. Knowing when to hire additional help and discussing options to relieve the workload can resolve unrealistic expectations, misunderstandings, and misperceptions.

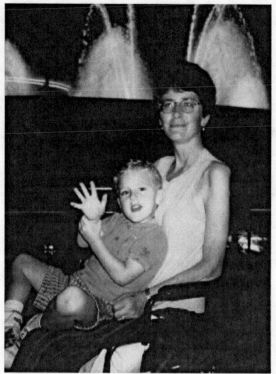

**Sandra and Nick at Disneyworld in 1998. Sandra can
no longer walk, uses a Bipap**

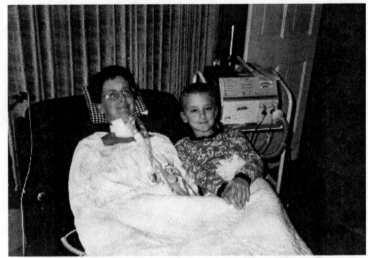

**Sandra, shortly after receiving the tracheotomy and
ventilator. Mother and son rest together**

Chapter 7
A Positive Life With Advanced ALS

"You can't do anything about the length of your life, but you can do something about its width and depth."—Shira Tehrani

The next three weeks were a blur. I knew this day would eventually come when I could no longer breathe on my own and I was prepared, at least by making my wishes known to Steve long before this date. I knew I must have a trach and ventilator, for Nick who was six, or I would die. It was that simple. I wasn't afraid of death, rather I felt I simply wasn't finished living. Though I knew what was involved in the transition from Bipap to ventilator as a nurse, I could never truly be totally prepared emotionally for such a life-changing event. This time it was happening to ME. But then ALS in itself is a life-changing event and I'd managed to deal with all its curve balls thus far.

My first evening at Inova Fairfax Hospital, October 31, Steve brought Nick to visit me in his Halloween costume. It was quite clear to me that if I had decided against more aggressive action I wouldn't be alive to see this simple act of childhood. I was still using the hospital's full face BiPap and since Nick was very accustomed and comfortable seeing me with a slightly different, smaller version of the facemask, it wasn't scary or new to him. But as the evening progressed I continued to struggle with my breathing, I whispered to my doctor with the little breath I had left, "Intubate me." I knew there was no turning back when I stated my wishes with these two simple words. I was intubated shortly after that under heavy sedation, I was glad I remembered nothing of the procedure. But with the tube in my nose going into my trachea and connected to a ventilator, I was no longer struggling to breathe. I relaxed and slept with the help of powerful sedatives. I knew the next step, a tracheostomy, would happen very soon. I was scheduled for the OR the next day to place a permanent trach in my neck so the tube could be removed from my nose. I really did understand what was involved in all this, after all I had worked with intubated, trached, and ventilated patients in the ICU at Fort Hood, but now I was on the receiving end. I was ready.

When I woke up I barely remembered what had happened and what would happen over the next couple days, whatever drugs they gave me had a successful amnesiac effect. But what I definitely knew was that I was breathing, easily. I slept. On day three I was stable enough to be transferred to the Washington, DC VA Medical Center and woke up from my drug induced slumber. For the first time I was alert enough to survey what happened to my body—I had a trach, ventilator, central IV line in my upper chest, arterial line at my wrist, NG tube in my nose to my stomach, and catheter in my bladder. But despite all this invasiveness I actually felt comfortable, my breathing was easy and no longer a struggle. The ambulance took me to the VA's MICU (Medical Intensive Care Unit) to continue my healing and prepare me for my life with a ventilator. This was my first hospitalization since my ALS diagnosis and I really didn't know what to expect.

The next three weeks allowed me to adjust to the ventilator under ICU supervision while the medical staff fine-tuned my settings. Some personnel thought the breath rate should be so low that it would force me to initiate a breath on my own to prevent my dependence on the ventilator, this was terrifying. Because of the nature of ALS I simply couldn't, the muscles needed to breathe were gone. Once these "trials" were over and the right settings were determined I was very comfortable. Being awake and alert now I wanted to communicate but I had lost my vocal voice when the trach was placed, no air moved over my vocal cords to create sound. With the assistance of a speech pathologist, we tried several different techniques without success. Maybe because of my muteness or because of my quadriplegia, I seemed in the periphery of decision-making with Steve speaking for me. He was making my desires known to all involved. At this point I didn't care, I passively accepted the circumstances. Eventually though, my outlook on my personal involvement in my care would change dramatically. But not yet.

My discharge planning began early and I was astonished to learn that the hospital had planned to send me to a nursing home in Baltimore more than an hour from our home in Fairfax, Virginia. This would be a death sentence for me. My whole purpose for living centered on living at home with Nick and being actively involved in raising him and Steve knew this. The issue boiled down to the fact that this hospital had never supported a patient going home with a ventilator. There was a steep learning curve for everyone in addition to wondering if they could even do it. I would be the first if they could pull it off.

Interestingly this MICU did not practice primary nursing or any continuity of nurses' assignments to the same patients, meaning I had a different nurse every day and every shift. It was impossible to establish any real rapport at all with any of them for more than twelve hours. Luckily respiratory therapy didn't work this way. By fate or something else, one particular respiratory therapist always seemed to be there when I needed him. He talked to me, he explained things, he eased my anxieties, he became my advocate. And I learned he was a Vietnam veteran, which explained why he comfortably called me Colonel. He remembered and respected that I was an active duty Army officer not so long ago despite what ALS did to my physical body. Clayton Worthy did more for me in those three weeks helping me to adjust to the ventilator than anyone else. And I'm sure when the discussions about the feasibility of discharging me to a nursing home versus home was debated, he supported what was best for me even though the hospital would be venturing into unknown territory.

From my perspective Clayton seemed to shoulder the whole responsibility of preparing me, my home, and my caregivers for a ventilator at home. Sure, there were others but a brief two-minute in-and-out visit was nothing compared to the extensive quality time Clayton made for me day after day. I felt he truly cared about me as a person. And so the training and preparation for my discharge home, not the nursing home, started and ended with Clayton.

I also made my desire known to have a feeding tube placed before my discharge. This had been on my mind throughout this hospitalization, I knew I couldn't continue to struggle and choke every time I attempted to eat. It was simply time for a feeding tube. I was being practical. During my entire hospital stay I had received nourishment through an NG tube, a tube in my nose that went to my stomach, it was terribly uncomfortable. The procedure to insert a permanent feeding tube took place in my MICU room under conscious sedation. Within thirty minutes the nasogastric tube was out and a new feeding tube directly into my stomach was in. What a relief. Once again I was more comfortable and the struggle to eat ended.

I was discharged a few days before Thanksgiving, the transition home went fairly smoothly thanks to Clayton and Steve. At this point I still let others make all the decisions involving my care, I was still adjusting to not only being completely paralyzed but now also a trach, ventilator, and the loss of my voice. I lived day to day, slept a lot day and night, and read with my automatic page turner. It was a mundane existence. I was physically alive but my internal spark was gone.

About three months after the trach and ventilator I had a serious conversation with myself. What was I doing? Was I happy? Where had my personality gone? What happened to my core values? I got mad at myself for letting ALS steal my spirit and sap my energy. It wasn't that I felt sorry for myself or felt pity, it was more apathy and indifference toward my life, something I never experienced in my healthy years. I got angry at my dysfunctional attitude and made a decision to reclaim and reinstate the person I always was. I was physically healed, now it was time to heal my spirit.

The first important action I took was to hire more caregivers who would be responsive to me and my needs. Maria only worked Monday through Friday and left in the early evening. The VA helped by providing an aide through an agency for the weekday evening hours but I still needed someone to help me on weekends. This was actually a big decision primarily because of the cost. I was already paying for Maria's employment and now I would be adding another part-time person. It wasn't cheap. After considering the costs and direct benefits to me, I knew this was the best choice as opposed to the current arrangement. I placed an ad in the Washington Post, interviewed, and hired an additional person, by myself. With more control of my care and now able to direct what I wanted to do when I wanted to do it, I started to feel in charge again. This expensive investment was well worth the benefits. The spark started flickering again.

Another important action I took was to learn what my computer could do for me. My setup was perfect and the more I used it the better and faster I became. I had no movement anywhere below my neck, not even a finger or toe, plus I had just lost movement of my head and neck. My computer setup with a motion sensor detecting movement of my cheek was my savior. I could move my cheek so I used it and used it hard. I had always been computer literate, now I became computer savvy. Computer access gave me the ability and more importantly the independence to do everything an able-bodied person could do.

The combination of having adequate help and discovering the limitless possibilities of my computer gave my spirit the boost I needed. I searched for, found, and reasserted my long buried personality. I reassessed the values and ideals I had always had from childhood and throughout my nursing and military career and put them back in the forefront of my life. These were the qualities of always looking for and accepting a challenge, being actively involved, and being proactive and positive. Then I finally accepted unequivocally that my life was forever changed and living in the past was destructive. For the first time I referred to myself as a quadriplegic, paralyzed, and disabled. This was an important forward step toward reclaiming myself, this time as the same person I always had been but with a different body.

My computer became my best friend. I reconnected with my long lost Army buddies who thought I had fallen off the face of the earth. I realized how negligent I had been in letting my friendships lapse and how important these relationships were. I can't explain why I temporarily severed these ties except that during the years of slowly becoming paralyzed I was totally consumed with my own slow demise that I couldn't involve anyone else with my problems. But despite what I had been through, I now felt ALS had maxed out what it could take from me and I started effectively dealing with what I had today and now. Even though my Army friends were assigned all over the United States and actually the world and not anywhere close to Virginia, I felt the closeness I once had on active duty with the Army's camaraderie. Reestablishing my friendships was important to reestablishing my dormant personality.

Now that I was using my computer every day for many hours I began searching for online people connections. I really didn't know where to start and knew nothing about chat rooms, discussion groups, or blogs. I wanted to talk to others with ALS to combat the isolation I felt. But where were they online? I decided to post a message on a general ALS group website and shortly I received a response from Ira in New Jersey who also had ALS. He told me about a chat room where folks with ALS hung out and invited me to join them. I had never been to a chat room and was very nervous about what to expect. Plus I couldn't type fast, after all I was using my cheek. But I took the plunge. I signed in and this began many long-term online friendships and continued healing my fractured spirit. This ALS chat room was very active and at any given time could have as many as 12 to 15 folks in the room, all in different stages of ALS and paralysis and a few of us with ventilators. I realized I had much to offer to those who were just in the beginning grip of paralysis and the nurse in me came alive. I felt the satisfaction, again, like when I worked in my profession. But my new online ALS friends also gave back to me, mostly in their discussions about simply living and living with paralysis. I was enlightened. I was touched. I was changed. My concern about my typing was completely laid to rest, everyone in the room was "typing challenged," as they called it, and we all understood. They introduced me to instant messaging so I could talk to family and friends online in real time. They told me about ALS message boards. And I learned that most of them used online banking to pay their household bills since ALS took their ability to write. This intrigued me. I had always been responsible for paying the bills but of course had to give this up many years ago. I looked into it and set it up. The rest is history.

I visited the chat room every day. Some friends I've had from this group for years, unfortunately many have also died, including Ira. That is the unfortunate nature of ALS. People live and people die. But the open and honest give and take of this group who all had ALS in common was invaluable. It gave me a new perspective, gave me new ideas, and showed me I could still be a nurse.

The possibilities for living according to my personal standards with an ALS-changed body were really unlimited, I just had to discover and develop them as a quadriplegic. I had always been involved with Nick's activities but now I completely immersed myself with every aspect of his life. In addition to always previously overseeing his homework, I now contacted his teachers by email, maintained correspondence, and set up parent-teacher conferences in our home. I began setting up play dates by emailing Nick's friends' parents until he was old enough to make these calls for me. When Nick wanted to become involved in sports, I found there was always the option to register online which I did. I planned his summer activities, registered him online for all his camps, and coordinated his transportation. I planned his meals, which my caregivers very willingly prepared.

I resumed running the household again including the bills, the meals, the cleaning, Nick's care, my care. I became an expert at online buying and began purchasing all our families birthday and Christmas gifts. During the busy Christmas season I also took responsibility for writing our annual Christmas letter and preparing our cards, learned to make labels on my computer, and of course solicited my caregivers' help with the physical tasks I couldn't do.

Managing my care independently was a challenge but I did it. I developed what I called Sandy's Black Book, a collection of resources about the details for caring for me, that my caregivers called the bible. In this three-ring binder I put everything they needed to know. Using my computer I created a medical personnel phone list, family member phone list, medication list, daily care routine, instructions to reorder my medicine, instructions to order my ventilator supplies, the steps to reinsert my feeding tube, general information about the ventilator and its alarms, how to safely transfer me, and much, much more. With many different people now caring for me and with my increasing difficulty verbally communicating, this provided a seamless, consistent, and easily accessible resource to help provide the care I wanted. My black book didn't happen overnight, many of the documents are detailed and required gathering outside information. But once in place, updates were easy.

Through the encouragement of some of my Army friends who were in regular contact with me now, I considered writing. This prospect had always appealed to me but I never seemed to have enough time in my busy military career. I enjoyed writing and now I not only had the time but the means. My first venture into the unknown world of writing and being published was a short article to a nursing magazine, which was accepted and well received by their readers. Little did I know where this first publication would lead me or what new opportunities would emerge. I wrote more articles for different nursing journals, the ALS Association, and other organizations. Because of these different publications, I was contacted by individuals to write additional articles and others asked for help with projects they were working on. I really enjoyed writing, I felt it was my opportunity to tell my profession and others with ALS about the nuances of the disease from a very personal perspective.

I was busier than ever, felt productive in all my projects, and truly enjoyed my life in the capacity I was accustomed to before ALS. But I wanted even more. After exchanging ideas with Nancy Colfax about our similar reading tastes, a neighbor I met through Nick's school who became a good friend, I tentatively started a book club. I say tentatively because I simply didn't know if it would succeed. I knew it wouldn't be a typical book club in many ways and I didn't know how people would respond to this. We would have to meet in my home every month, I wouldn't serve lavish refreshments, and participants would have to be comfortable with a ventilator-using quadriplegic leading the discussion. Once a small group of five or six ladies indicated their interest, I started by asking their preferences for the types of books they had interests in. They indicated American biographies, historical novels, and classics. All the planning and coordination was really quite easy, I had become as adept on the computer as any able-body. The Fairfax County public library had their complete catalog online so I could easily read reviews, summaries, awards, and number of books available before selecting them for our reading list. It worked perfectly. The book club has had a steady membership from day one. Occasionally a new person joined our discussion - some have stayed, others felt too uncomfortable. We are a lively group from diverse professional backgrounds and interestingly everyone has some kind of military affiliation—Army, Air Force, and Navy. We aren't a lightweight book club and I'm teasingly chided for some of the tomes I select, such as Fountainhead, Ivanhoe, Eleanor Roosevelt, and The Agony and Ecstacy. We have been a group of friends for more than six years now.

So how do I manage and host a monthly book club which centers on discussions when I can't talk? The simple answer is it takes planning and preparation. I communicate with members between meetings by email when necessary. I begin working on our six-month reading list months in advance and it continually changes until I finally distribute it, then it's final. But this part is fairly easy because of the online catalog. Of course the biggest challenge is communicating during meetings. When the book club was in its infancy, I still had complete control of my mouth movement even though I produced no sound over my vocal cords because of the trach. However I could generate certain sounds from air just in my mouth. By listening very carefully in a quiet room I could actually be understood. As time passed and the thief continued to steal what precious abilities I had left, I eventually lost the movement of my lips. Again I turned to my computer. I began to use my voice synthesizer. I could type and speak responses to spontaneous questions which was slow but worked. But more importantly I could prepare phrases and questions ahead of our meetings that I could easily speak when the time was right. So even though my ALS continued to progress, I found solutions to the obstacles and the book club survived and thrived.

I met many health care providers through the VA's Home Based Primary Care program I was part of. I found I had much in common with several of the nurses, they had been military nurses too. There is a camaraderie and friendship that easily develops because of shared values, familiar experiences, and simply a certain personality. One nurse in particular was the Director of this program, a retired Navy Reserve officer. Susan Jackson wasn't your typical remote administrator, she seemed to be involved in everything including being the president of the local chapter of Sigma Theta Tau, the Honor Society of Nurses. Because of Susan's friendship and persuasion I transferred my membership to Kappa Chapter at Catholic University in Washington, DC. I had transferred my membership many times in my military career when I was geographically reassigned and had never really been actively involved. But now Susan wanted me to fill a vacancy on the board. I normally would have jumped at an opportunity like this but now I had to consider my physical limitations, I would never accept such an assignment unless I could do it according to my high standards. With Susan's persistence and assurance that all business was now being conducted electronically, I agreed to give it a trial. I stayed for two years in my position as their membership involvement person then was reelected by the membership for another two-year term. During this time I also wrote an article published in their national magazine, Reflections on Nursing Leadership. I wouldn't change this experience in any way, I met so many professionally active nurses and was asked to participate in other projects as a result. The interesting part was that most members, having never met me, had no idea I was a quadriplegic on a ventilator. It's not that I hid the fact, rather it never came up in my work.

Additional opportunities presented themselves mainly through my involvement in other things. For example the International Ventilator Users Network invited me to serve on their Consumer Advisory Council, which I accepted. I also wrote several articles for their quarterly newsletter Ventilator Assisted Living. Another example of getting more involved is, the invitation extended to me from the national ALS Association to join their newly formed VA Issue Team, I accepted this as well.

I mention all this because of the possibilities, the opportunities, out there. Remember I have absolutely no movement below my neck, have no movement of my neck, use a ventilator, can't swallow requiring frequent oral suctioning, and ALS is now moving up my face affecting my lips and expressions. I'm not wallowing in self-pity nor do I lie in bed all day. What makes me get up each day? Attitude. I have a certain personality that makes me pursue a challenge, even though it was buried for a short time. It was bound to resurface, and it did. And part of this attitude is a mentality that I'm not sick, I just can't move.

There is a significant triad of factors that support my attitude, actions, and outlook on living every day with advanced ALS. These three imperative factors are adequate help, computer access, and necessary equipment. I will address my caregivers in a later chapter and I already discussed the way my computer opened the world of possibilities to me. I have certain equipment that makes day-to-day living comfortable, that without it I would definitely be physically miserable and therefore mentally distraught.

Sleeping through the night is critical to both physical and mental health therefore a good specialty mattress is essential. I tried several types before finding the one that afforded me the comfort and support I needed for uninterrupted sleep and prevention of pressure sores. A cheap flotation mattress really isn't enough for someone who can't move at all nor is a turning mattress appropriate because it provides no head support when neck control is lost. The mattress that best meets my needs is a constant airflow system with an adjustable firmness/softness control. I have never had a pressure sore and I don't need to be wakened at night to be turned.

How important is a shower? Imagine going without one for days, weeks, or months then you can appreciate its importance for someone with ALS. When the master bathroom was renovated, a roll-in shower was a major addition replacing the small conventional step-in shower. But with complete paralysis, no head control, and a ventilator, the logistics of making it work smoothly had to be worked out. My toilet chair, which fits over the existing toilet, also serves as my shower chair and is rolled into the shower in tandem with my wheelchair which holds the ventilator on a shelf below the seat and remains located just outside the shower curtain. The handheld showerhead allows more precise water placement so the trach doesn't receive a direct hit. The ventilator tubing can safely get wet because it's a closed system. I absolutely love my showers twice a week. After my hair washing and body scrubbing is done, I simply sit in the hot stream enjoying the moment.

Having the right tilt-able, cushioned wheelchair is important but so is having a comfortable recliner chair. The electric controls allow precise positioning, changing position to shift pressure points, and raising the chair for my caregivers to work more safely. Personally I find the recliner chair more comfortable, easier to do my work from, and logistically always in the right place.

I love the comfort of my home and actually feel little need to venture out, but when I do, having an accessible van is the only way. I guess I feel I have seen so much and been exposed to so much in my Army career that I am quite content with the comfort of my home. Going out requires planning and coordination. First, certain supplies and equipment must accompany me. Second, the place I am going to must be reconnoitered to be sure it is wheelchair accessible. Third, all equipment must be fully battery-charged. And fourth, I must anticipate frequent oral suctioning and my inability to communicate in any way. My most frequent outings have been to Nick's sports events, my parents home in Pennsylvania, and the annual Walk to Defeat ALS in Washington, DC. So for this phase of my life I have become a homebody. It is my decision and I'm happy with it.

The notion that quadriplegics have little useful existence and vegetate day to day is an idea that is infuriating. Granted I need assistance with all my activities of daily living but certainly not with my mental functions. I get up at 7:30 AM every morning. After a bout of passive range of motion exercises in bed, I am up in the wheelchair and head to the kitchen. I sit at the kitchen table to read the Washington Post while I have my breakfast of Osmolite by the feeding tube. Late morning I go back to the bathroom for my morning care and get dressed. By noon I am ready to sit in my recliner chair, have lunch, and set up my computer to begin my work. I schedule all my appointments, conference calls, and other business at this time. I work independently with my computer whether it's for the book club, nursing honor society, bill paying, caregiver payroll, monthly employee tax filing, gift buying, research for articles, email, and much more. When I finish my work for that day, I read. I always go to bed at the same time, 11 p.m.

My mind is always active, engaged, and involved even though ALS took my physical body. Because I have the right tools, my computer and dedicated caregivers, I can fully exercise the one ability ALS can't take—my mind. Lying in bed all day, living in pajamas, vegetating are not options. As depressing as ALS can be, I can't see the benefits of succumbing to its atrocities. The paralysis of ALS is certainly different from other types of paralysis in that it continues to progress, there is no ending point. It takes the muscles to breathe, the muscles to swallow, the muscles of the neck then slowly moves up the face taking lip movement and facial expressions. But it can't take my mind, attitude, and personality. Because I have a choice how I want to live, I chose to live life not to live impending death.

Lessons Learned

- Plan and communicate your medical intentions.

Anticipate the medical interventions you may need, don't be caught unprepared. With ALS, I knew a feeding tube and a ventilator were on the timeline. Rather than be surprised when that time did come, I knew exactly what I wanted and had communicated my desires to my husband. In the same way, it's equally important to complete and communicate your living will or advanced directives, establish a power of attorney, and have life insurance policies in order.

- Keep the right attitude.

Did you see and feel the shift in my attitude? Don't let this happen to you. Catch the drift toward negativity early. I was able to pull myself up by the bootstraps by sheer determination. But if you can't, ask for assistance. It helps to know what information and resources are out there to help you achieve the level of living you desire. Also talk to others who have figured it out, first hand knowledge is indispensable. There is the I-give-up attitude and then there is the catch-me-if-you-can attitude. ALS can't steal your attitude but it will try. Having the right information helps. And it's why I wrote this book.

- Hire caregivers.

Recognize early when it's time to hire help. There is a big difference between feeling like you are "bothering" a family member who is busy with something else and asking a paid caregiver who is there only for you. The freedom to do what you want, when you want, eliminates the restraints that may hold you back from fully pursuing the activities that are important to you. Let others help who do this for a living.

- Make your computer your best friend.

Regardless of your limitations, a computer can be adapted to keep you connected. My computer uses an infrared motion sensor placed beside my cheek with an EZKeys software program and a voice synthesizer but there are many many options. The key is to get it and use it. I can't stress enough how critical a computer is to stay in touch, keep current, and get involved, from reading online newspapers to instant messaging, reading ebooks, and gaming. If you don't know computers, now is a great time to learn. But don't miss this opportunity to develop your friendship with your computer.

- Acquire the right equipment.

For someone who is paralyzed, positioning and comfort are tantamount. That's why the right equipment can make the difference between being miserable and being content. The two places I spend the most time, my recliner chair during the day and my bed at night, are ideal for me. Identify where you can benefit the most from improving your physical comfort because it will directly affect your mental well-being, then comparison shop, talk to others, and make your purchase.

- Get involved.

There are plenty of opportunities to put your skills and interests to work. I found that one activity often led to another and doors opened in unexpected ways. I used my background as a nurse to keep myself employed. Whatever your area of expertise and interest, reach out, ask, volunteer. It could be a professional organization, a charitable group, a university, a church, politics. Find your cause and you will find satisfaction.

Stuban with her son, Nick, age 8.

First Quarter 2004   Reflections on Nursing LEADERSHIP   29

Sandra and Nick in 2004. Sandra is completely paralyzed and uses a ventilator

Chapter 8
Friends, Family, and a Cat

"Good friends are like stars. You don't always see them but you always know they are there."—Anonymous

ALS can easily cause anybody to withdraw. The transition from being completely strong and healthy to slowly becoming paralyzed is terrifying no matter how you look at it. When that person is a confident and independent individual, the response to ALS can be to simply deal with it alone away from the critical, pitying, un-understanding eyes of others. That's what I did, at least at first. I had no desire to burden anyone with my troubles so I dealt with it alone. I know now I should have chosen the other path.

The importance of friends and family cannot be stressed enough. These are the people who form the backbone and infrastructure of the support systems that help make living with ALS more bearable and enjoyable. In fact, research studies support the premise that social contacts contribute to a greater sense of well-being in everyday living. The saying "no man is an island" is certainly true. Then factor in the anxieties and fears associated with ALS—body changes, impending paralysis, limited mobility, loss of speech, choking, difficulty breathing, loss of independence—and the importance of friends and family skyrockets. There will naturally be a process of self-elimination of certain acquaintances. Some will be negative, others uncomfortable, and still others can't be bothered with someone who is "different." Unfortunately, or perhaps fortunately, you really discover who your true friends are at a time like this. The good news is that the people who surround you now are genuine, the ones who truly care.

The first two years after my ALS diagnosis I continued to work. The physical signs were still subtle at that time and my friends who knew my personality and my work reputation were there as always. They knew me and ALS didn't change these relationships. Then our family moved when I medically retired from the Army and Steve received military orders to Bethesda, Maryland since he was still on active duty. Frequent moves are part of the military, you pack up and make new friends. I had done it my whole professional life. But this move was very different. We moved to Fairfax, Virginia with me in a wheelchair.

Several factors compounded my initial isolation. First, we moved to an area where we knew nobody. Second, we had no family in Virginia. Third, I was not working for the first time in my adult life. Fourth, I was still adjusting to the effects of ALS. And fifth, I didn't want to bother anyone with my difficulties. So I coped alone. The whole concept of literally being friendless was foreign to me. I was so accustomed to the close support and camaraderie of the Army network. Several questions went through my mind in the first months in our new home. How can I make new friends when I don't work? How can I meet people when I can't walk and don't go out? How will people see me, like a cripple? How will people know who I really am? They can't possibly know me as the athletic, driven, promoted-early Army officer I was. The frustration was that my physical body no longer responded to everyday challenges though I still could mentally.

After the initial disaster of trying to do this alone, on my island of one, I started reaching out. And since I was limited physically, my first new friends were online, an unfamiliar, and sometimes unsettling, experiment in finding cyber friendship. As I mentioned I eventually found an ALS chat room with the help of a fellow PALS (Person with ALS), Ira, who died about a year later. There I met all kinds of people who also braved the effects of ALS. Some struggled tremendously with the changes, others completely accepted their new lifestyle. That's where I met Dave. I can say he changed my perspective on living with ALS in many ways at a time when I was still struggling myself. Here was a man three years younger than me, diagnosed with ALS nine years before me, and used a ventilator two years before I was diagnosed yet he seemed to harbor no ill feelings and lived his life fully. Through our online correspondence I learned he had been a coal miner, lived in West Virginia, and had been a successful amateur boxer until two years before his diagnosis. He lived at home with his wife and two teenage children. His personality was such that he was very easy to get to know—open, honest, sarcastically funny, and at times blunt. After a period of time we exchanged photos so we could associate a face to our discussions during our instant messages (IM). And fitting to his personality his photo showed him in his wheelchair with a ventilator dressed in a superman outfit. This was Dave.

We talked about everything from ventilators and trachs to current affairs and very personal topics. Even though I have never met him, he is a very good friend. I am convinced that everyone with ALS needs a friend with ALS, no one understands our plight better than someone who has been there himself. At least for me someone like

Dave showed me an alternative perspective and attitude that made absolute sense. His attitude was refreshing and infectious yet he lived with ALS since he was 25. He was a fighter and a survivor. I knew I was too.

I still had no local friends in Virginia, I had no means to meet people. I missed my military buddies, work, and the Army. These were the people who really knew me. I was crazy for thinking I could go through the biggest trial of my life without them. I found my closest Army friends through email and we simply picked up where we had left off years before. Many wanted to call to talk to me but I had no voice. I wanted to talk to them so bad too but it was just one more frustration I had to deal with and accept. So we talked by email. It was such a pleasure to learn that every single one was promoted from Lieutenant Colonel to full Colonel over the years and eventually retired. Laurie, a PhD researcher and nurse midwife, retired in Washington state. Patti, a former hospital inspector general, retired in Ohio. Jennifer, my former supervisor, settled in Colorado then later Massachusetts. And Karen, still on active duty, recently served in Iraq then Korea. My best friends were scattered all over the earth but I still had the closeness of their thoughts and conversation through the internet. In their own way they each encouraged me, pushed me, and forced me forward. Some asked tough clinical questions to help solve current issues. Others encouraged me to pursue a doctoral degree online. And many pushed me to write. I guess the overwhelming benefit of these long distance friends was that they accepted me as I was without pretense. To them I was still the same person. The emptiness of my new ALS existence was slowly eroding and was being reinvigorated by my old friendships.

About the same time I reconnected with my long-time "pen pal" from second grade, my longest friend. Our friendship had always been unique. Roberta lived in

Michigan and I lived in Pennsylvania when we began correspondence as a requirement for Brownies at the age of eight. We hit it off and as we grew up we always stayed in touch despite my frequent military moves. But we lost contact for years after my ALS diagnosis, the same as I had done with my other friends. When I did receive that first email from Roberta after so many years, I decided it was time. I told her everything. Instead of being repelled, which is always a possibility, our bond became stronger than ever. She made ALS her cause too. Our friendship picked up where we left off.

I made another long distance reconnection when the new Pastor of my church back home in Pennsylvania, St John's Lutheran church, contacted me to make visits here in Virginia. I must say I was skeptical. Even though my parents were very active there, I almost felt like an alien. I had been physically away due to my military assignments and now ALS, I couldn't imagine anyone remembering me, or caring about me, despite being their organist more than 30 years ago. Plus the Pastor would have to travel 300 miles round trip. Despite my reservations, I consented. Surprisingly, at our first meeting, we clicked. Pastor Tom was young, personable, and talked to me like there was nothing wrong with me. I detected no pity, no disgust, no hesitancy. This was important to me early on as I was just coming to terms with my paralysis and physical changes. We easily talked while he caught me up on all the people I had once known and the many activities the church was involved with. He assured me that many members did in fact remember me as their organist. We talked and prayed, he gave me communion, and we jointly agreed to meet every two months. As he talked about our visits to the congregation, I began receiving cards, emails, and gifts from the people I had once known so long ago. I started feeling connected again to my childhood church that had always been there for me and now reached out across the miles. Several significant events happened after Pastor Tom started this bimonthly ritual. Some members expressed an interest in traveling with him to see me. One was Ray, I had served as an accompanist for his singing family when I was a teenager. During these visits we reminisced and he sang for me in his ever-brilliant baritone. Another was Carol, who took a personal interest in fundraising for ALS research. With her outgoing personality and can-do attitude, she mustered many donations for the annual ALS walk that I had become involved in to support research. These visits filled a void I felt since moving to Virginia away from my physically close friends.

I was touched when Pastor Tom emailed me one day to tell me his Sunday sermon would be about me, the theme was choice in the face of adversity. As I read the script he sent me, I realized the impact I do have on other people and the strength of character I must indeed have without fully recognizing it myself. It took this indirect, subtle act to help me realize I was well on my way back to reasserting my lost persona. I probably benefited more from his sermon from 150 miles away than many in the pews that Sunday.

Another event Pastor Tom kept me apprised of was the decision to build an addition to the 225-year-old historic structure to house an elevator to make the church completely accessible. I found this intriguing not only because of my present situation but also because this very rural country church identified the high tech need and acted on it. Pastor Tom told me about the negotiations, showed me blueprints, and shared with me the obstacles and setbacks. And when the elevator project was finally completed and the dedication date established, I decided to attend. This was really a big decision because I rarely made overnight trips simply because of the logistics involved. I made the arrangements to spend the weekend with my parents after covering all the bases. Then I had to prepare myself for seeing church members who last remembered me as a spry young adult and had probably never seen a quadriplegic and a ventilator. I also had to prepare myself emotionally for the impact of seeing the physical church again and the organ I once played. I later learned that the week before the dedication, which I would be attending, Pastor Tom gave a children's sermon about looking past a person's physical differences and seeing their actual character. Then he talked about my paralysis, the trach, the ventilator, the need for frequent suctioning, my inability to talk, and the computer I use to communicate. Of course his message was meant for everyone to prepare them for my extreme physical disability. That was just the kind of sensitive, thoughtful, understanding man Pastor Tom was.

When the day arrived I used the new elevator to enter the sanctuary on the second floor and felt completely welcomed with no sense of apprehension or uneasiness from anyone. After the Sunday service and dedication, the congregation met in the social hall on the main level for a covered dish luncheon. Here I set up my computer so I could talk with whoever wanted to chat. During the course of this special meal, I believe every person present came to talk with me. In addition I was frequently surrounded by a group of young children who were fascinated that I operated my computer with my cheek and could make the computer speak my words. They asked simple and direct questions typical of their innocence, and I loved it. Following the social, I took the elevator to the balcony on the third level to see the organ. I knew my eyes would tear as I remembered the old days and the things I love that I can no longer do. The whole day had been emotional as I knew it would be. The 150-mile drive back to Virginia gave me plenty of time to review the day's many events and mull over their impact.

Returning to the seat of childhood memories can be trying even for able-bodied folks, just as I was returning to a familiar place and familiar people as a physically changed person. I wanted to smile and chat and catch up and slide on the organ bench and run through the mountain like I did as a kid. But I'm not a kid any more and I now have a completely different adult life. The key was being able to enjoy those memories without dwelling there and to live in the here and now with my current circumstances.

Through my reassociation with my distant church I found a group of people who cared about who I was despite the physical changes. Granted, they knew me before ALS but it didn't seem to matter. I just wanted to be treated like a normal person, not pitied, not tiptoed around, not looked at with disgust. They treated me like the Sandy I am and I appreciated it. A church and its people can be a wonderful source of unconditional inspiration.

I had plenty of long distance friends and I knew how important they were to me. But I still had no local close friends who could only know me as a person with ALS. I think it takes a special person to see past the paralysis and trach and ventilator and suctioning to enjoy the company of a person trapped in a dysfunctional body. I certainly wish society as a whole was more accepting of people with disabilities but we're not there yet. This person was Joan. She worked at the VA hospital and made her first routine home visit to me to evaluate the agency home health aides they were providing. When I first met Joan I was using a BiPap and still able to use a scooter to get around in the house. She was the consummate, caring, confident nurse with an engaging personality who had a no-nonsense approach to her work. The patient's well-being was always her highest priority. In getting to know each other over subsequent visits, I learned she had been an active duty Navy nurse then active in the Reserves. We became best friends. When she moved to another job within the VA, of course our friendship endured. She was the first local person who I felt truly knew me, and the professional career I had that was cut short. I welcomed our intelligent, stimulating conversations. Joan reminded me of the many Army nurse friends I had that were scattered all over the globe. She stopped in to see me frequently and often asked my professional opinion on clinical issues. So when she met and decided to marry a Canadian gentleman, I went to their wedding. By this time I was completely paralyzed and using a ventilator but Joan made sure the church and reception hall were completely accessible to me. It was a beautiful wedding and they were so happy together. But at the same time I knew I was losing another friend to geography. Joan was moving to Canada with her new husband.

The idea of a book club churned in the back of my mind. I looked into several local existing book clubs but they just didn't accommodate my physical needs plus I was sensitive to imposing myself on a group of new people who may not be prepared or accepting of my disabilities. In addition, most local clubs met in someone's home which are not accessible to a wheelchair. Then I looked online for book clubs and entered several book discussion chat rooms but was disappointed. My only option, if I was to have a meaningful discussion of books, was to start my own club. But I was really at a loss about membership because I knew so few people locally and those I did know worked. This is where Nancy helped. I learned she was married to an active duty Army Colonel in our neighborhood. She understood the nature of the Army's frequent moves and would stop in when she could after taking care of their three school age children. But it was with Nancy that I brainstormed about forming a book club. She invited several women she knew and I invited several of Nick's friend's mothers I knew. Even though the initial response was positive it faltered from lack of interest. We persevered. Nancy invited my next-door neighbor, Janet, who I knew through Steve but had never met. And she in turn invited another neighbor, Judy. I invited an old friend from graduate school, Ruth, who lived 45 minutes away and surprisingly she was interested enough to make the drive once a month. This formed our early group.

These incredible ladies were remarkable in many ways. They met in my home once a month to have intelligent discussions without elaborate refreshments or pretense. I was one of the group despite my physical differences. Probably one of the most important features of this group was I felt they came because of their common interest in discussing books not because of their particular thoughts about me. And this interesting, unique, and diverse group of professional women was not only mature in their ability to accept disability but also contributed to rousing and sometimes differing opinions at our meetings. They were always invigorating conversations.

As years passed and the book club continued meeting every single month, the group gelled and bonded in special ways. The interesting thing is that every woman had a strong personality and unusual life experiences that made every meeting sometimes unpredictable. Nancy was a lawyer who now stayed home with her children. She had moved frequently with her active duty Army husband. Ruth was a retired Air Force nurse who I first met at graduate school at the University of Kansas. She now devoted her time to politics and mission work. Janet once worked as an elementary school teacher then raised their seven children while moving frequently with her active duty Navy husband. They retired and moved to the home beside ours more than 30 years ago. Judy, who lives across the street, had worked was NASA while her husband served in the Air Force. It was never intentional but we all had military backgrounds in some way.

Several new people attended our meetings but most didn't come back. I can speculate why. It's unfortunate and sad that I was probably the cause. But two new people joined our core and added yet another dimension to the diversity and depth of our discussions. I met Desiree during a routine home audit by the Virginia Employment Commission. She had an outgoing personality and seemed perfectly comfortable with my paralysis and ventilator. A rare trait. After our business was over, she told me she had googled my name and found an article I had written describing the book club. She asked me about it. I thought she was being kind. Then she asked me about it again later and I realized she was sincerely interested. I gave her the details and invited her to join us. She did and has been an integral, active member ever since.

Zilpha had been my speech pathologist at the VA for many years. When she retired we stayed in touch, I always enjoyed her company. I thought she would be a great asset to our group with her doctorate, prior active duty Air Force service, and extensive career experience, so I invited her. She was hesitant, she was very busy in retirement. But after she came to one meeting as a trial, she couldn't stay away. She hasn't missed a meeting since.

This monthly meeting of the minds is stronger than ever. I look forward to every session. Every one of the women who comes to my home every month to discuss books is special simply because they have been able to put brain power above my obvious physical limitations. I am part of the group. I am not treated any differently. And amazingly only Ruth knew me before ALS, everyone else met me after I was paralyzed using a ventilator. I have seen many reactions to my disabilities from avoidance to obvious discomfort. These ladies are classy in their straightforward acceptance of a severely disabled woman who became a friend.

I literally had to recultivate my inner circle of friends at the very beginning of my diagnosis when we moved to Virginia. It was essential but particularly difficult when I was also trying to cope with the slow paralyzing effects of ALS. I think the biggest change in my outlook occurred when I was "maxed out," that is ALS couldn't take much more. When I was completely paralyzed and using a ventilator, I rebuilt my major friendships. And though these friends are not always physically near, I know they are there.

My parents have always been my pillar of support. From the first day when I told them I was diagnosed with ALS to today when ALS has stolen my whole physical body. The amazing part was their ability to know when to step forward and when to step back. They didn't crowd me or suffocate me with tears or pity or shame but were always there when I needed them. I know the whole idea of their daughter having ALS was devastating to them. They knew me and my personality so well, they knew I had a very successful and promising military career cut short. In that sense I felt I had disappointed them. But there is no turning back the clock. And just as I accepted my unchangeable failing strength, they also moved from wishing for the past to the realities of the here and now. Their love never wavered.

There are probably a gazillion examples of all the little and big things they have unselfishly done to help me in some way since my diagnosis. And since I am a person not to ask for much, they would often take the initiative on their own, always in their non-assuming way, never overwhelming. How do parents know how to do this so well?

Dad and Mom still live in our home in Elizabethville, Pennsylvania but they make the 150-mile trip to Fairfax, Virginia as often as they can, usually every two to four weeks. Even in retirement both are extremely busy. Dad still works part time in his butcher business he sold many years ago to another young ambitious butcher. And Mom is involved in many church activities and social clubs. Despite being in their 70s, now they are as active and spry as ever. I respect their wealth of information they gathered from a lifetime of experiences.

Dad remains the perpetual problem solver and a man of action. When he saw the make-shift way I propped up the newspaper to read every morning, he came up with a better solution without even saying what he had in mind. On one visit he simply presented his invention—a homemade wooden newspaper stand using dowels, a tilted frame, and moveable supports. It was definitely worthy of an official patent.

Another dilemma I faced was the logistics of overnight visits to their home in Elizabethville. Even though it is a ranch style, there is one large step into the house. Dad easily solved this with a wooden ramp. The other major showstopper was I had to have a safe means to use the toilet. I used a special toilet chair at home but it was large, non-collapsible, and difficult to transport. After eyeballing this chair, Dad simply built me one. It was elevated, had arm supports, a high back, and head support plus it was easily disassembled and removed. It worked perfect.

I had always struggled with different tables when I sat in my recliner to work on my computer or read using my page turner machine. I tried side tables, overbed tables, and tables slid in place from the feet but all had problems. Again, without saying a word, Dad took measurements of my recliner. It was obvious he was formulating some kind of plan, a mental blueprint. At their next visit he presented his latest invention—a portable wooden desk that fit perfectly and snugly over the arms of my recliner chair. It was the ideal solution yet something I could never buy anywhere. It was solid, lightweight, practical, and easily removed when I didn't need it. And all this from the man who used his hands and mind his whole life to solve problems in his successful butcher business.

Dad always seemed to identify and eliminate the small irritants that I couldn't resolve on my own. He made small wooden ramps so my wheelchair would more easily clear the door thresholds to go outside. He made a small platform stand to secure my computer sensor I used next to my cheek. And he was always available for small household fix-its. How does a daughter say thank you to her Dad for all this and more?

Mom was the organizer and cleaner, as she has always been. On their weekend visits she would put order to the small areas of disarray. With Nick growing like a weed, she kept his outgrown clothes in check, which was a constant issue. She thoroughly enjoyed decorating the house for the season at hand whether it was Easter, Thanksgiving, or Christmas, and it looked great. She included Nick in helping with special activities that I would normally have done with him before ALS like making birthday cakes or baking Christmas cookies. She always tried to maintain a sense of normalcy amid my lifestyle as a quadriplegic. The amazing part was that she was never overbearing or excessive, every small and large act was needed and much appreciated.

Mom also coordinated the family gatherings in our home three times every year at Easter, Thanksgiving, and New Year's day. Both my sisters, Teresa and Sheila, and their families would come for extended stays. That meant at least 13 family members, and often their friends, were sleeping and eating here. Mom is in her glory in this environment. She plans all the meals, spends many hours in the kitchen, and often has games lined up. She is famous for her Easter egg hunts where she hides plastic eggs with money inside in our backyard. Every year it seems some are never found. These holidays give me a chance to catch up with my sisters who are busy with their own careers and families in Pennsylvania. But I never have to worry about anything on these eventful holidays, Mom always has everything under control. As usual.

After years of adjustment and uncertainty in our marriage, Steve and I settled on a lifestyle for him that he was most comfortable with. I managed my own affairs, he managed his own. He wanted minimal involvement in my care so I used paid caregivers 15 hours a day and Steve "covered" my night hours when I often slept through the night. He decided to live in the lower level of our ranch style home. But despite living separate physically, we had reached a practical and realistic understanding about the workability of our marriage. We communicate through email and make joint decisions regarding Nick and home projects. I mention this because of the necessity to be flexible and accepting of unusual arrangements after an ALS diagnosis. Sure, I would have preferred a traditional marriage but ALS stole this too. I couldn't dwell on the past wishing for an Ozzie and Harriet relationship, instead I accepted a nontraditional marriage arrangement I couldn't change, just like ALS.

One recent Christmas, we made an important addition to our family—an adorable calico cat. Nick had grown from the typical pets of gerbils and hamsters and had befriended a local outdoor cat. He wanted a cat desperately, as kids can state their case so dramatically. I loved animals but I had unanswered questions about animals around the ventilator. So I posed the question to an online ventilator discussion group I belonged to. These are people who used ventilators because of high level spinal cord injury, polio, ALS, and more. I guess I expected warnings, horror stories, and negative responses but every response was absolutely positive. I learned that many ventilator users do have cats and they shared their heartwarming experiences and stories. I was pleasantly surprised by the intense relationships these fellow ventilator users had with their pets. With all my anxieties put to rest, we told Nick he could get a cat. After deciding we would get his pet from the local shelter, I began looking at their website which showed pictures and gave descriptions of each animal available for adoption. Several times every week I showed Nick the choices. One day I saw a cat that tugged at my heart strings and showed Nick this one year old calico female. I immediately emailed Steve and said we had found the one. Steve and Nick went to the shelter that Saturday and as Nick immediately fell in love with her, another family was deciding between this cat and another. Luckily Steve made his intentions known without delay and after an exhaustive and professional interview process, we had adopted Keoni. She adapted quickly to her new home. Nick absolutely loved her. I watched to see her curiosity and response to my ventilator tubes, the ventilator, and me, a person who doesn't move or pet her. She was the perfect lady and bothered nothing other than a few sniffs. I still wonder what she thinks about me, though everyday she naps beside my legs on the recliner. And Nick puts her on my lap and physically lifts my hand to help me pet her. I thoroughly enjoy her company and antics, she is entertaining in so many ways. A pet is a perfect companion. I certainly can now understand the attachment and love my fellow ventilator user friends expressed about their pets, I felt the same emotions for Keoni.

When the ALS Association first began their signature fundraising event, the Walk to Defeat ALS, I trashed the flyers. I had no interest. But as I extended my network of online and local friends, it dawned on me how important it was for me not only to attend the walk in a wheelchair with a ventilator but also to do my part to raise money for ALS research. So I registered a team online, Sandy's Vision of Hope, and put the word out by email to my family and friends. This was the one time, the one event, where everyone came together because of what ALS did to me. Since I became actively involved in the annual walk, each year the walking team grew and our team contributions grew as well. I enjoyed the planning, the correspondence, and the pulling together of so many different people for this common cause. The morning of the walk we all met at our home for the trek to Constitution Garden on the Washington, DC Mall. My local friends, some distant friends, friends from my church in Pennsylvania, my book club friends, and my family all converged to physically support me by walking with me. It's incredible to feel this strength of purpose, the pride of collecting donations for such a worthy cause. I always provide an after-the-walk brunch buffet in our home, with Mom's never-ending help, as my way of saying thank you. It also provides an opportunity for my diverse group of friends to meet each other and for me to use my computer to talk to all my supporters. During the walk itself I have no means to communicate, but everyone understands that and patiently waits for my computer to be set up. It's this annual show of force because of ALS that simply touches me. The love of family and friends is irreplaceable.

Many times family and friends are taken for granted like breathing, swallowing, and smiling. But when the essence of life is stripped and stolen as in ALS, it causes you to rethink those things that truly make us human—companionship, intelligent conversations, unconditional love. I lost these things for a while as ALS devoured my body but I soon recognized their importance to maintain my mental and emotional health. As much as ALS wanted to force me into a rut of isolation, and I succumbed for a short time, I persevered from pure determination and attitude. The cycle completes itself—when love and companionship are given, they are easily reciprocated. That's what makes us human, even in adversity.

———

Lessons Learned
- Nurture your friendships.

I made a big mistake by letting my friendships lapse. Fortunately I realized my error and reached out to my established friends and sought new friends both in my new community and online. Stay in touch, your computer makes it easy. Welcome and invite your friends to visit. Friends offer so much more than simple companionship, they also bring a sense of normalcy to a lifestyle that sometimes feels alien.

- Get involved with your church.

New and existing friendships abound at your local church. I have found a dearth of pity and an abundance of genuine support and appropriately placed concern. Just by being involved generally generates a circle of caring people you ordinarily wouldn't come in contact with. It's an additional source of support.

- Start a group.

When I began relying on a wheelchair, I realized people's homes were not accessible to me any more. Multiple steps, narrow doorways, or cluttered rooms were showstoppers. That meant I had to invite my friends to my house. I found an easy way to do this on an ongoing basis was to start a monthly book club. But there are many different options for a gathering of your friends limited only by your imagination, such as a monthly movie night, Bridge, Bible study, or Trivial Pursuit. It's not only fun but it also keeps friends close.

- Love your family.

I am closest to Dad and Mom and their love and support are unconditional. I stay in contact with my sisters, niece, and nephews by email, IM, and occasional visits since they all live outside Virginia. Accept and cherish the love of your family near and far in whatever capacity they support you. Some may be able to be there for you physically every day, others may be there for you emotionally at every moment because they do not live physically close. Whatever the situation, love your family.

- Adopt a pet.

A dog or a cat is a perfect constant companion. Pets seem to have an unexplainable awareness of those who are weak, hurting, physically limited, and sick. It's difficult to describe the change I felt when Keoni became a part of our family. She brought her subtle calm yet playful nature to our family and I'm sure she sensed our love for her. Pets are so loving and are a wonderful source of unconditional love and affection.

- Find a cause.

I made ALS research my cause. Every year I call upon my family and friends to help support fund raising and they always respond. Whatever your cause, it gives you a reason to be excited about upcoming events and to draw together your family and friends to support this common cause as well. It's very satisfying and touching to see everyone pull together for one specific reason that benefits you.

Sandra with her team, *Sandy's Vision of Hope*, 2008, Walk to Defeat ALS, Washington, DC, Constitution Garden

Chapter 9
The Caregivers

*"Any act of kindness, however small, seems big in the
eyes of the receiver."—Aswin Narayanan*

There are certain people who literally became my
arms and legs when ALS took my strength and
movement. These are my caregivers, people devoted to
helping me when I could no longer do even the most basic
activities myself. Without them I was mired in a
frustration of futile, tiring attempts to maintain my
independence. With them I could achieve my seemingly
simple activities of daily living despite the loss of my
coveted autonomy. Even though initially I mentally
fought the inevitable need for human help and with it the
loss of my independence and privacy, physically I knew it
was not only more practical but safer. As my needs
changed from minimal assistance to complete care with
the ventilator, I also had to change and adapt my thinking
about how I viewed this new requirement, the need for
permanent caregivers. Just as I eventually accepted ALS
as a new lifestyle, I also accepted the numerous caregivers
into my life and my home and entrusted them with my
well-being.

When I began to rely on others more and more, I
naturally wanted them to treat me with the same dignity
and respect they would treat themselves. Being a friend,

having similar values, and feeling like a member of the family was something I desired since they would be intimately involved in many very personal aspects of my life. But again I wondered if this was a realistic aspiration. After all, this was a paying job. Would a paid caregiver view this as "just a job"? I also wondered if I could be a boss, the payer of services, the receiver of services, teacher, and friend all at the same time. It's a delicate balance. Certainly some paid caregivers see this as purely a job with set duties and strictly set hours, while others are truly caring individuals who simply do what needs to be done. I have seen just about everything in the many years I have relied on caregivers for help, some good and wonderful, others stressful and unsafe. But regardless, I know I must have help with every basic activity.

When we first moved to Virginia, I could barely walk with limited use of my arms and hands. With Nick just 2 ½ years old, in diapers, and a ball of energy, I realistically couldn't stay home with him alone safely while Steve worked full time. As much as we initially resisted the need to hire someone, we also recognized its necessity. I placed an ad in the Washington Post having absolutely no idea what to expect. At that time I required only minimal assistance myself but needed more help with Nick since I couldn't do even the simplest things, like grasping the Velcro on his diapers to change them, opening a refrigerator door, and basically keeping him out of trouble. There was actually a small response to this ad, which I realized I had placed over the Christmas holiday. Steve and I interviewed the interested individuals and hired one particular person on the spot. She was originally from Guatemala, loved children, and was young and lithe. Little did I know at the time that she would eventually stay with me more than five years. These five years became the most life-changing years of my life when I went from being mobile and independent to being a ventilator dependent quadriplegic. Maria saw me through these very tough times.

Maria worked the hours that Steve was away at work. Initially she spent most of her time with Nick doing the things I could no longer do—dressing him, bathing him, preparing his meals, playing outside, changing his diapers. And she helped me a little as I needed it. As time progressed, Nick needed less and I needed more but Maria adapted. Interestingly she had no medical experience except a Red Cross CPR certification that she had needed for her previous nanny positions. But the important thing was that she was willing to learn what needed to be done and readily accepted my changing physical needs and her changing role. I was very fortunate to have her.

I first started using a BiPap when Nick was almost three and Maria and I learned the nuances of the equipment together. Other changes started happening with my walking as well, I could stand but I could no longer take steps. But this didn't deter Maria. Now using a wheelchair, Maria would take both Nick and I to the park, the library, grocery shopping, and more. Even during the hot summer months when we got Nick a small inflatable pool for the backyard, she put on her bathing suit too and chased him in the yard and around the water in the pool. She never balked or complained. She was like a member of the family.

Nick was becoming more independent and I was becoming more dependent. When he no longer needed help to dress, I needed more. When he no longer needed help to bath, I needed more. When he no longer needed close supervision, I needed more. My legs were no longer reliable. One day when Maria stepped out for a few minutes, I tried to stand up by myself from a chair but my legs failed me and I fell and of course couldn't get up. Nick came running to me and in his youth, about three or four, assured me it was OK and sat with me on the floor until Maria returned. Maria's response was incredible. Maybe aided by a rush of adrenaline, all 100 pounds of her scooped me up off the floor like she was Mr Universe.

Just as my legs were failing me, my arms followed suit. As degrading as it was, I couldn't lift my arms to feed myself, so in addition to preparing our meals, now she also fed me. And as time progressed, it took me longer and longer to eat. I had to be very careful because I easily choked on my food, ALS was taking the muscles I needed to swallow. In addition to being patient with me while I struggled with each meal, Maria was quick on her feet when eating became an emergency. I can't count how many times she did the Heimlich maneuver on me to dislodge food that had inadvertently entered my trachea. In that sense she literally saved my life many times. This was the way things were changing and she changed with the times without complaint.

When I was hospitalized to get a trach, ventilator, and feeding tube, a higher level of medical care was required and again Maria rose to the occasion. Even though she cried the first time she saw me in the hospital with the trach and ventilator, she had the fortitude, intelligence, and compassion to learn everything to safely care for me at home from suctioning to changing the ventilator tubing. In addition, she also had to learn how to use my feeding tube and give my medicine through the tube. Instead of throwing up her hands in frustration, she simply did what was necessary. Considering how drastically her role had changed from caring for a toddler to caring for a quadriplegic on a ventilator, she was an incredible individual.

About a year and a half after I had the trach and ventilator, Maria told me it was time to go, she wanted to be a nanny again. I couldn't blame her. She had spent more than five years with me doing things she had never imagined but doing them well. She was with me as I went from walking, talking, and eating to complete paralysis, a feeding tube, and ventilator. These were the days when my physical abilities changed almost every day, it wasn't an easy time. But never again would I have another caregiver stay with me as long as Maria.

This was a critical transition for me after having Maria as my primary caregiver for so long. Though I was using a combination of privately hired help and agency assistance through the VA's support, Maria was my sole dependable principal caregiver. The people who followed her had all kinds of personalities and idiosyncrasies; some stayed a day, others several years. The disruption of constant new people was like a revolving door, it was tiring and frustrating. I just wanted some stability. I wanted people I could trust, depend on, and love like a family member. But I found a dizzying collection of "health care providers," both privately hired and from the agency, who amazed and disappointed me with their lack of a decent work ethic. I feel compelled to share some of these experiences, in no particular order.

I had several people steal money from my wallet. Of course I could never prove anything but I know who they are.

On a first day of training, one person lay on a bed and went to sleep. She was not asked back, needless to say.

I have heard more cases of car trouble, flat tires, and family deaths than is practically possible as excuses for not going to work.

One person even filed a lawsuit against me after I let her go after six weeks. I had to physically appear in court during the winter months in zero degree temperatures. After hearing testimony from both sides with Steve speaking on my behalf using power of attorney, the judge ruled in my favor.

On a second day of training after observing the technique to give my shower, one individual said he didn't want the job unless he was paid more. He didn't come back.

One individual used her cell phone constantly, even while giving my shower. When I asked her about it, she said she had six sisters and had to talk to them every day. I suggested she talk to them when she was off work, but she became irate saying I didn't understand her culture.

One day another individual took off her shoes and socks, dug around between her toes and toenails, then replaced her shoes and socks. When I asked her to wash her hands before suctioning me, she laughed and said she didn't know I could see her.

One individual told me that helping me with Nick wasn't in her "job description."

And yet another individual, after he completed his training period and was scheduled to work alone the next day, didn't show up because "it was too much work." I was stranded.

As a nurse and a member of this health care profession, I could never understand these attitudes and behaviors. Since I have been in the position of requiring assistance and depending on caregivers, I have often reflected on my own hands-on nursing care I provided while working in the ICU for patients in comas, on ventilators, and with a gazillion tubes and wires. I know I paid attention to every detail, put the patient first before anything else, and respected my patients and their families. Because of my background I also understand infection control and the basic needs of a total care patient. But I have also been a head nurse in two hospitals so I can easily spot those who come into my home who say they are "nurses" yet lack the essential mentality of truly caring. Sometimes I wonder if my standard is too high. No, it isn't. I think back to all the nurses I have worked with throughout my nursing career in Philadelphia and the military, there are those who go above and beyond, would do anything for their patients, and simply exude caring, then there are others who count the minutes before their shift is over and dash for the door. It saddens me when I encounter yet another caregiver who is successful at only giving the health care professions a bad reputation.

Since being on the receiving end of care and obviously receiving this care in my home, I have become very interested in the standards for home care so I have taken advantage of the wealth of information available online and in professional journals. I know I'm not off base when I expect a certain level of competency and shared philosophy about what home care entails. I have had the privilege of knowing several caregivers who were true "care" givers and believed and practiced the concept of holistic home care.

Terry was the first male nurse to work with me. He was an RN with extensive hospital ICU and homecare experience and had just finished his master's degree in informatics. Not only were his clinical skills exceptional, he also viewed homecare as caring for not only me but also my home and family. His views and approach were a breath of fresh air. He assessed not only me but also my environment and acted on his findings. For example, the water from my showerhead was very weak when the water pressure everywhere else was strong. One day he brought his plumbing tools, took apart the showerhead, and removed an O-ring causing the problem. Waalaa, instant water pressure. My showers improved 100 percent.

Another example was he questioned why I didn't have a printer set up to my computer despite the hours I used it when I had a new printer still in the box downstairs. After finding it, checking it out, and buying the necessary cables, he connected and set up the printer. My ability to communicate just improved.

And yet as another example, about this time I was having difficulty closing my mouth. He had an idea to make me a chin support to help me close my mouth. One day he brought a portable sewing machine, material, and elastic and made me a support. He was always looking for ways to improve my quality of life and was successful.

There were many other instances of Terry seeing the big picture and going above and beyond what the minimal requirements of the job entailed. He was a true professional who could best be described as a big cuddly teddy bear. I was very fortunate to have Terry for even the short time he was here. He had accepted a promotion to a management position. But his ethic and overall approach to homecare restored my faith in my profession.

I found Jeanette when I placed an ad in the Washington Post looking for help. With the revolving door of caregivers coming through my home and the many disappointments, I didn't know what to expect. But she has been a true gem in so many ways. Our mutual appreciation for each other has evolved into a sister-like relationship, which is evidenced by her working with me more than four years, so far. Jeanette came to me with a lifetime of homecare experience as a nursing assistant and had seen just about everything. After learning the nuances of the ventilator, she was comfortable with every aspect of my care. My home became her second home.

Jeanette's philosophy of homecare meshed with mine, which gelled our personal and professional friendship. She saw the big picture. If something needed to be done, she simply did it. Everything was in her "job description." She cared for me like she would care for herself and she respected my home like her own. She would take me outside when it was nice, go with me to Nick's sports games, and make the trip to Pennsylvania.

In addition to caring for me, she kept the house in order and cooked for Nick. When others complained about "all the work," Jeanette just saw a need and took care of it. A comment she made to me one day I'll never forget, she said if I wanted a shower everyday she would happily do it. I know it doesn't sound like much to the average person but this small act of kindness meant the world to me. And most importantly, she would never leave me stranded. When others pulled a no-show or had excuses for missing work, she came and made sure I was taken care of. Incredibly she never missed a day of work or called in sick in all the years she has been with me. She has often told me angels watch over me. Yes, I believe it because she is one of them.

It's hard to describe the transition that must take place, both physically and mentally, to accept the need for assistance with absolutely everything I do, activities that any able-body person simply takes for granted. At the stage I'm at now I can't breathe without a ventilator, I can't eat without a feeding tube, I can't move without someone moving me. The functions others do for me are critical to my well-being, health, and disposition. Consider also that every caregiver has her own style, which is understandable. As an able-body person you have your own way of combing your hair, putting on deodorant, brushing your teeth, even wiping your butt. Imagine someone different doing these things for you everyday, everyone doing them slightly different, and nobody doing them exactly how you would. This is where I especially learned patience and tolerance. I certainly appreciate that others are willing to do these things for me so being hypercritical of minutiae really serves no purpose. Another example of the importance of practicing patience and tolerance is one caregiver thought he was doing something special for me by cracking my knuckles everyday. I had never cracked my knuckles in my life and didn't like it now but I never said a word rather than deflate his sense of doing an act of kindness.

I have experienced so many different caregivers that I have discovered they fall into one of three categories— those with a light or feather touch, those with a normal touch, and those with a heavy almost rough touch. Most caregivers provide my care in the normal category but I can remember those very few by name who have the lightest touch because it is so preferable. I have often wondered if the "heavies" are rough with themselves as well when doing something personal. I'm talking about jerking movements when positioning me, pushing too hard to suction, rough handling while dressing me, swiftly moving my head or extremities. So many times I wanted to offer these caregivers my chair for 24 hours so they could experience first hand the effect their touch has on a person. I have to admit it's scary sometimes. That's why when my normal and feather touchers care for me I appreciate their calm hands-on approach. Fortunately the heavy handers are few but they do have a profound impact and leave a lasting impression.

It's unfair to give the negatives so much attention when there are so many good people out there doing good deeds. To me, it's easy to recognize those who chose nursing for the right reasons. These are the people who seem to know that little things mean a lot, and believe me they do mean a lot. In nursing and homecare it's not just about doing assigned tasks, anyone can do that. It's about massaging atrophied legs that don't move any more. It's about taking a little longer to comb my hair. It's about picking up a dirty dish Nick left. It's about rubbing feet that no longer touch the ground. These are the acts of kindness that set people apart and make them special to the receiver of their ministrations.

Caregivers are an essential part of my life now, without them my quality of life would be nonexistent. As

I have learned patience, tolerance, and acceptance with different personalities, varying techniques, and loss of home privacy, I have also learned gratitude, appreciation, and recognition of every small act of kindness that I used to take for granted.

Lessons Learned

- Hire wisely.

I live in a large metropolitan area where the response to my ads was varied and unpredictable. But what I learned over the years can be applied in all circumstances— determine the reason the individual wants work in homecare, look at certificates and license, check public court records, make reference checks. Yet all this is not fail proof. Any new employee should be watched carefully initially as they are given such independence in your home. Unfortunately because of the "poor" performing individuals you must be more vigilant with all new employees. But when you do find a gem, it makes it all worthwhile.

- Learn patience and tolerance.

I currently have six paid caregivers covering 15 hours a day, seven days a week. Each has their own personality, touch, and technique. You can never expect things to be down exactly how you would do them yourself if you could. Therefore you must learn to accept, adapt, be patient, and be tolerant or you will make yourself crazy. When I went through the process of thinking this through years ago, I rationalized, what difference does it make if someone puts on my deodorant differently than I would or brushes my hair differently or even wipes my butt differently, if the end result is the same. I am saner and just thankful I have someone who willingly does these things for me.

• Maintain your high standards.

Just as you adapt to caregiver differences, you must also be firm about things that really matter to you and communicate that to all your caregivers. There are simply some things I won't compromise on. A few examples are, I don't tolerate anything being dropped on the floor for infection control reasons, I expect diligent hand washing, and I insist that lights are turned off when not being used. It's not unrealistic to establish house rules, after all it is your home.

• Develop mutual respect.

When you do find those caregivers who mesh with your personality and ideals, you will find it's easy to take care of each other. Not only friendships develop but also mutual respect. For me these are the people who go the extra mile and genuinely care about me as a person not just as a body or a reason for a paycheck. Developing these bonds is actually easy when that respect is reciprocated.

Sandra and Nick, 2003

Chapter 10
The Art of Parenting

"There are two lasting bequests we can hope to give our children. One is roots; the other is wings."—Hodding Carter, Jr.

What exactly is parenting? Are there different expectations for the able-bodied parent and for the disabled parent? Can a quadriplegic be an effective mother? These are some of the questions I asked myself as I progressed through the stages of paralysis. Fortunately along the way I was able to develop a solid concept and confidence of parenting as a mother with severe physical limitations. After much thought, I was able to organize my abstract thoughts into words for this chapter. To me, parenting is providing a secure loving environment and a foundation in moral living, which guides the development of a confident and well-adjusted child into a productive and successful adult. Thinking of this definition from both an able-bodied and a disabled perspective, since I experienced both, there is certainly nothing there I can't do now as a disabled mother. And in putting this definition into practice I have found that "thinking outside the box" helps in finding unconventional solutions to obstacles and accepting impossibilities as facts of life simply reduces frustrations.

As any parent knows, being a parent requires great responsibility and the right attitude, not only about being a mother but also about life and living in general. I have always felt strongly that ALS must be second to my son, he comes first. My outlook had to be bright, my attitude positive, my approach to obstacles teachable. That's how I dealt with ALS's encroaching paralysis in the early stages as a parent when the loss of abilities was ongoing, I didn't let it interfere with my important job of being a mother. Of course it's impossible to ignore the obvious activities that comprise most parents' days with their children. I can't play ball, I can't be a "soccer mom," I can't make lunches, I can't bake cookies, I can't volunteer at school, I can't, I can't, I can't, can't, can't, can't. That's a negative trap I refuse to fall into. Instead I focus on what I *can* do, not what I can't. As James Dobson has said, and titled one of his many books, "parenting isn't for cowards." And I say that's true for any able-bodied parent as well as for me with advanced ALS.

To talk, most easily, about raising my son while living with ALS, I have identified three distinct phases— ages 0–6 when I was going through the most physical changes and could still talk, ages 6–12 when I was completely paralyzed and used a ventilator, and finally the teen years. I don't claim to be an expert on childrearing but I certainly have a different perspective as a career woman who planned her pregnancy, loved her son intensely, then coped with the devastation of ALS shortly after his birth. I knew I couldn't be a coward to my son and certainly not to ALS. And I wasn't.

The time from birth until age six is most commonly known as the impressionable years. When I was diagnosed with ALS just five months after Nick was born, I didn't know what the future held for either of us. I didn't know if I would be alive after two or three years as my neurologist predicted for me or if I could be the mother I always envisioned myself being despite the paralysis I knew would slowly come. One thing I knew for sure was that regardless what happened to me because of ALS I refused to let it interfere with my relationship with my son, the frustration and anguish I may have felt while adapting to my physical changes was my burden not his. I also knew he learned from my example and watched the way I responded to activities I wanted to do, once could do, but could no longer do.

When Nick was eight weeks old he started daycare at the hospital where I worked, I was still active duty Army and expected to continue my career. I really felt no conflict in balancing my roles as Army nurse and mother. The arrangement was perfect. Even the arrival of ALS five months later didn't upset this balance. In fact through Nick's first year there was no discernable evidence of physical weakness, meaning I did everything exactly as I wanted without limitations. But around his first birthday and about the time he had learned to walk and run, my weakness became evident and started affecting what I could do for and with Nick. But this was my problem not his.

The first time I fell lifting Nick was from his highchair and meant I had to immediately change how I did this. Nick of course thought the fall was an adventure and laughed as he lay on my stomach. But I no longer took the risk of lifting him here or anywhere else. Instead, for meals I removed the tray and he climbed into his seat to eat then climbed down when he was finished which he thought was much more fun. I quickly discovered that at this phase of ALS a major requirement for me was the necessity to adapt, find alternatives, and implement creative solutions as issues arose.

I spent much time playing on the floor with Nick but eventually getting up and down constantly became impossible. That simply meant I had to be more organized. Before sitting on the floor I gathered everything I could possibly need such as an array of toys, books, snacks, wipes, diapers. Once I was down I stayed down because to get up was a major challenge. To get up from the floor without assistance I had to crawl on my hands and knees, with Nick following suit, to the nearby stairs and slowly slid my butt up each step until I was high enough to stand on my own. And Nick watched.

I knew Nick was always very astute which was reinforced by an incident that happened when he was about 18 months old. One weekend day both Steve and I were busy with something in our home while Nick was playing. When I checked on him he was nowhere to be found, we searched the house but no Nick. When Steve opened the door to the garage he found the garage door open and when Steve ran to the driveway he spotted Nick on the other side of the street running down the sidewalk in a diaper and a t-shirt. After investigating how this could have happened we saw that he had moved a stepstool below the button to open the garage door, something he had seen us push everyday we went to work and daycare. This incident certainly opened my eyes a bit more about what he saw and what he understood, even at this young age.

From the time Nick learned to walk, he ran. He ran everywhere. One day when he was about two he came running to me in the living room and threw his arms around my knees, something all toddlers do everywhere with their moms. The combination of his impact and my loss of leg strength and balance caused me to fall straight backward. This was a significant fall for me and I lay there for several minutes catching my breath and regaining my senses. I learned I had to sit down in the presence of a rambunctious toddler. It never happened again.

In addition to the floor, my lap became a favorite playground. Nick and I played many learning games here and read many books together. Quickly it became his "job" to hold the book and turn the pages when I couldn't lift my arms to do it myself, a real act of discipline for a very active toddler.

Nick stayed in the hospital's daycare for two years and four months until I medically retired and Steve had travel orders for an assignment at Bethesda, Maryland. Nick was fortunate to have the same wonderful young lady caring for him during this whole time. Lisa also had her son with the group of five children she was responsible for and Nick and Timmy quickly became best friends, his first friend at the ripe old age of 18 months. His experience in daycare was very positive and afforded him exposure to valuable social interactions and outside rules.

By the time we moved to Fairfax, Virginia and hired Maria, I couldn't safely be alone with Nick, a horrifying thought for a mother. Maria assumed his physical care while I continued educating this young boy. But I couldn't help but wonder if I was less of a mother because I couldn't change his diapers or give him baths or prepare his meals myself. Would this affect his development in some way because I didn't do these things? After the initial adjustment of accepting the need for a paid outsider to do what I couldn't, I realized these thoughts were ridiculous. Maria was wonderful with him and spent much time outside with him running, playing tag, chasing each other, and simply expending his overabundance of energy while I watched. Sure it broke my heart but again I was determined not to impose ALS on my son.

Being as perceptive as I knew he was, Nick certainly knew I had certain limitations but he never asked about it. I often wondered when I should tell him and what I should say. I always thought I would wait until he asked but he never did. He simply took everything in stride, amazingly. But one day I felt the time was right. Nick, about three, was sitting on my lap playing. I began by saying I can't do many things other moms do because I have no muscles. He looked at me and said OK and kept playing, completely unfazed. I didn't say any more, I thought maybe I was wrong to bring it up and that Nick was too young or not quite ready. I decided to wait until he asked questions.

Nick was ready for preschool, he had been accustomed to the daycare routines with the accompanying social contacts while we lived in Hawaii. So when he was three I enrolled him in an excellent local program for two years. He was back in his element, around other kids and a structured learning environment. Frequently I would accompany Maria to pick him up at midday but go a little early so I could talk to his "teachers" and just observe him in his new surroundings. One of the first times I came, Nick ran to me full of excitement followed by several of his little buddies. I'm sure I was a curiosity to them because I was in a wheelchair. In one big long breath Nick said, "This is my mom she has no muscles, Mom watch me!" And he runs off with his friends to show me what he could do on the indoor jungle jim. All I could think was, wow. Not only did this perceptive little boy hear every word I had said weeks earlier but it was also obvious that my physical differences from other moms had no impact on his relationships with others. He wasn't ashamed or embarrassed because I was different, I was simply his mom. I was so proud of him that day, my heart overflowed with love.

About the same time I searched for a church for Nick to attend. I knew it wouldn't be the kind of family environment I grew up with in Elizabethville at St John's Lutheran church or what Steve had in the Catholic church in Connecticut but I had to do the best I could given the circumstances. I found a local church, Bethlehem Lutheran church, and emailed the Pastor about our situation—that we recently moved into the area, that I wanted Nick to become active in their church, and that I wouldn't be able to accompany Nick because of my ALS. Nick was welcomed with open arms when Steve dropped him off there every Sunday. His formal spiritual learning had begun.

Nick went through a phase where he was obsessed with spiders, they fascinated him in every aspect. One day while playing on my lap, and out of the clear blue, he said, "Mom, I think I know how to cure your illness. We let a spider bite you and the poison will kill the virus." Yes, he said the word virus. Well, I was flabbergasted. I wanted to encourage him for thinking of such a novel idea and said the researchers were thinking about similar treatments and he was very smart for thinking of this. It was obvious his developing thoughts took him places he didn't always share with anyone.

Full-day kindergarten at the local public elementary school started for Nick when he was five. Maria walked him to the bus stop every morning and returned to wait for him every afternoon, he seemed so small with his big backpack compared to the older kids. He was so excited to start school plus he discovered that his friend David from preschool was also in his kindergarten class. At home I supplemented what he was learning at school, my lap was still a favorite place. When he got too big for my lap, he would squeeze into the chair beside me. And though at this point ALS had taken all my movement, when Nick hugged me, I whispered softly in his ear, I am hugging you back. He understood my love despite being physically unable to display it.

About two months into first grade when Nick was six, I went into respiratory distress and was hospitalized for three weeks for a trach and ventilator. The next phase of ALS began whether we were ready or not.

I don't have a first hand account of Nick's response while I was gone for those three weeks but if his actions during his visits to me were any indication, he took it in stride like he always had the past six years. Trying to imagine the change from full-time BiPap to trach and ventilator from his perspective, I could understand how he might see this as an improvement. With the BiPap, part of my face was obscured with a thick tube that ran from my nose, between my eyes, and over my head. It was held in place with a head harness and straps over my cheeks. The ventilator was one tube to my neck. With his young eyes he saw my face unencumbered. The BiPap and ventilator machines were performing the same task. Nothing much had really changed.

Probably the biggest change though was the loss of my speaking voice. ALS had not yet taken my voice but the trach prevented air movement over my vocal cords. So I figured out a way to articulate each word without normal sound and use air in my mouth along with my tongue to make sounds for many consonants. Nick understood every word I said. Sure, I couldn't call to him across the room but I could still talk to him when he sat with me or was close by. Our reading regime changed from me reading books, to him doing the reading.

Nick's elementary school years expanded his independence and I encouraged this. Without a voice I had to change my primary mode of communication with others from using a phone to using email, which often required advanced planning. I arranged his play dates this way and carpools and transportation to his other evening activities. And when the annual parent-teacher conferences were held, each year I emailed his teacher to request a meeting in our home, which every teacher accommodated.

I made every effort to afford Nick all the opportunities available to kids with able-bodied moms. In my mind it was unfair to limit Nick because of my limitations. With Steve's support, I encouraged cub scouts, sports, the church youth choir, and summers full of camps. I took care of online registrations and payments and arranged transportation whether it was Steve or other mothers. Nick was involved in everything he had an interested in and had his circle of friends, nothing was denied him because of my disability.

I began participating in the annual Walk to Defeat ALS in Washington, DC when Nick was in third grade. I explained what it was all about and at this time Nick began referring to my "illness" as ALS. I didn't quite know how Nick would react to the ALS walk and seeing others with disabilities from the same cause but I prepared him the best I knew how. This first walk was a success with Nick beside me every step of the way. After the excitement of the day calmed to a gentle roar, Nick sat beside me and asked this poignant question: "Mom, why were you the worst person there?" Nick had seen many people in wheelchairs but nobody who couldn't move at all or had a ventilator. As much as my heart pained for him at that moment I answered the best I could. I explained that many people as advanced as me chose to stay home, that's why it's so important for me to show others what can be done with advanced ALS. He seemed satisfied but again I knew he was taking in much more than he let on.

Nick always eagerly helped me with little but important things, like scratching an itch or removing a stray hair on my face. When new caregivers were being trained, he listened and learned more of the nuances of my care and when he got older he actually served as a resource to them when they forgot something. He was the expert at setting up my computer and sensor, reading my lips, and problem-solving ventilator problems like loose or disconnected tubes. Many times I wondered, if my eight-year-old son can do this why can't educated adults? I never pressed Nick to assume any of my care, I believed he was still a kid and I refused to rob him of his childhood because of me. When Nick was about eight or nine, he asked to do my tracheal suctioning. He had seen it done a gazillion times and heard the instructions to others, he wanted to do it himself. It only took one supervised trial because his technique and understanding of the principles were absolutely perfect.

When Nick turned twelve another significant change occurred, this time with Nick. He wanted to make his own choices and decisions with less interference from his parents, it was time to step back a bit. Hoping he would rely on all the moral teaching of right and wrong, I became more an advisor, hoping to guide him rather than "dictate" his actions. This was actually a difficult transition for me. I enjoyed the cuddly little boy I was so close to but the reality was he was growing up and testing his wings. I had to respect that and even encourage it.

In sixth grade, the class was given a science project. Each group of four was assigned to write a paper about a disease, which included interviewing a person with that disease and doing an oral presentation to the class. Nick's group included three of his very good friends so I was extremely pleased when he suggested, and his group agreed, to do ALS. We arranged a sleepover one weekend for all the boys where they could also interview me. I decided to prepare some opening remarks with basic information about ALS using my computer's voice synthesizer then let them ask their questions. When I was ready I called Nick and his friends. They stood around me like little reporters with their pens and tablets in hand. When I began, using the voice synthesizer, their eyes grew wide and asked how do you do that? They took notes while the computer spoke my words then they asked their questions, I encouraged them to ask anything at all on their minds, and they did. I was so pleased with their attentiveness and interest, I felt I had made an impact on four young boys and their views of the disabled. But I was especially proud of Nick because even in his group of peers in early adolescence he never shied away from acknowledging his Mom with her severe disabilities.

Nick began to take sports more seriously, especially his interest in running and football. I had always encouraged his sports involvement and tried to attend when logistically possible but Nick knew I couldn't attend every game and maturely accepted that reality. But the games I did attend were so rewarding mostly because of Nick's enthusiasm with my presence.

Nick had the typical pets growing up, first gerbils then hamsters. When he was twelve he decided he wanted a cat after befriending a local outdoor cat. Since adopting Keoni at the animal shelter a week before Christmas, the two became inseparable. As Nick would run through the house, Keoni was right on his heels with her tail held high. And he always carried her with him when he sat beside me to discuss things or would put her in my lap then raise my hand for me to pet her. I thoroughly enjoyed seeing the bond between these two.

When Nick knew I was writing this book, he became very interested in contributing in some way. So I emailed him specific questions that he answered in writing, of course between his video games. These are his thoughts as a twelve-year-old teenager.

When do you first remember I had an illness?

When I was three, walking and running around the house.

When I couldn't walk any more, what did we do together?

I remember playing with puppets.

Do you remember when I could walk?

The only thing I can remember is you moving around on your scooter.

Do you remember when I could talk?

I can remember you talking to me but not the words or how it sounded.

What do you remember when I went to the hospital for the trach and ventilator?

I cannot remember anything about that.

How do you feel about the ventilator?

It is what makes you breathe, nothing special.

When your friends came over to play, what did you tell them about me?

Most of the time they didn't say anything and I thought it wasn't a big deal, I didn't tell them anything until I was eight or nine.

How did you feel when I missed a basketball or football game?

I feel the same as if you were there.

Do you think I'm different because I have ALS?

I don't feel you are any different from anyone else, you have emotions and everything else adults have.

There are still several years of high school before Nick exercises his ultimate freedom and leaves home as an adult. Though I couldn't perform the physical aspects of being a parent, I was always available and hopefully instilled the qualities to be a hard-working, respectable, ethically-responsible adult. Because I didn't chauffer him to all his activities, because I didn't personally prepare his meals, because I didn't tuck him in at night, because I wasn't active in school PTA, does that make me less an effective mother? Absolutely not. But I was able to provide him an environment that encouraged certain qualities that able-bodied mothers couldn't, such as respect for the physically challenged, an ingrained sense of helping, compassion, and an appreciation for people who look different. And though I can't move or talk, I have found ways around the typical parenting activities to provide an unconventional, yet effective, loving environment to raise a young growing son.

Lessons Learned

- Put your child before your disability.

Nick always had priority before and after my ALS diagnosis. I made sure my physical difficulties did not negatively impact and impede his growth. Rather, his exposure to my disability made him a stronger and more well rounded young man. Don't be so consumed with your adversity that it interferes with your job as a parent. It's an attitude, it's an outlook, it's an approach that your child can sense. Use your disability as an advantage rather than a detriment to raising your child.

- Use your limitations as teachable moments.

Children are incredible sponges, they absorb every sight and sound. I saw this demonstrated very clearly with Nick as early as 18 months. Rather than hiding or trying to disguise your difficulty, put it on full display. These are your teachable moments, use them to your advantage. A child learns by observing your responses to adversity and obstacles, teach him well. And remember that your child sees and understands more than you might think.

- Focus on what you *can* do.

When there are many things you cannot do that an able-bodied parent does, it serves no purpose to dwell on it. Exert this energy on devising an alternate plan of attack. It may not completely quell your deep-seated desires to do what is now impossible, but it will give you great satisfaction when you do what is within your abilities. Know what you can do then do it with gusto.

- Let your child help you.

As early as 3 years of age, Nick wanted to help me. And I let him. A mother-child bond is very strong and only strengthened by an adverse situation. I never insisted or demanded Nick to help me, rather he initiated his actions on his own. Don't stifle or inhibit these acts of love. Encourage and appreciate them and your child will grow up with an ingrained tender touch and a caring heart.

- Return your child's unconditional love.

Regardless of your situation, your child will love you with unbounded energy. I sometimes questioned myself about what kind of mother I could possibly be as a ventilator-using quadriplegic and that somehow I was depriving Nick of key maternal acts he deserved. I was so wrong. There is a love that withstands and perhaps strengthens in unusual situations. Never doubt your capacity to love and return your child's unconditional love with an abundance of affection.

Chapter 11
A Survivor's Attitude

*"Come to the edge, He said. They said, We are afraid.
Come to the edge, He said. They came. He pushed them
and they flew."*—*Guillaume Apollinaire*

I have been known to be stubborn. I have been known to have a strong work ethic. I have been known to rise to a challenge. And I have been known to get things done now rather than later. I can't prove that these qualities and values I grew up with and practiced throughout my professional career made the difference in my outlook toward living with ALS but I believe they made a significant contribution. But still I have often wondered why 50 percent of people diagnosed with ALS die within three years and why only ten percent live past ten years when we all go through the same paralyzing effects. I have ideas and I question some of the explanations I have heard.

The speed of progression of ALS is slightly different for everyone. Some advance very quickly, others very slowly. Some begin with bulbar symptoms affecting breathing, swallowing, and speech, others begin with weakness in the limbs. But regardless of the rapidity or initial location, the ultimate outcome is the same—total paralysis. So I don't see this as a factor.

With the average age of diagnosis being 55 and many diagnosed much earlier (I was diagnosed at 38), ALS is notorious for dealing its punch in the prime of life, often with children at home. Why don't more people punch back? I am sometimes confused by the passive acceptance of death by paralysis without considering alternatives for living a new and different lifestyle. .

Perhaps some people merely fulfill their doctor's prescription of preparing for hospice and death. Without effective treatments to stop or reverse the progression of paralysis, some doctors unfortunately paint a picture of doom and gloom instead of encouraging a fighting spirit using today's technology and establishing strong support systems. When a doctor tells the newly diagnosed they have two or three years to live, as mine did, I suspect many resign themselves to this fact without question. However in my case I was stubborn, I forged ahead without his guidance and support. I am convinced doctors wield enormous influence on their patients in forming their initial impressions of life with ALS that last, whether positive or negative, whether to fight or succumb, whether to ultimately live or die too young.

Too often ALS is viewed as a terminal disease rather than as a long term chronic condition that can be managed with today's technology. Sure, there is no cure, just like many other medical conditions. ALS must be confronted with the right mentality, the right attitude, the right fighting spirit.

When dealing with ALS or any other unchangeable or devastating event, I have found a formula that has worked for me. It's simply the four A's—Accept, Adapt, Attitude, aggressively pursue Ambitions. It's a mentality of survival that defeats ALS.

Acceptance is the first big step. As unbelievable and shocking the news, you can first grieve then you must find a way to ultimately accept it. As much as you want to deny the reality and think this terrible thing can't happen to me, only someone else, the fact is it did happen to you. Describing the actions of Jews in death camps during World War II, Viktor Frankl recognized the need to accept their situation and find purpose to survive. We can learn a lesson from this tragic event on survival. An easy way to help accept a bad diagnosis is to be informed, learn everything you can about ALS. Knowledge is power. Even though much of what you read about ALS is depressing, it's imperative to be informed and prepared. And finally, as difficult as it is, talk to others with ALS. The best ways are to contact an ALS Chapter and ask to be put in contact with someone who also has ALS. I know this works because I have made myself available to my local Chapter specifically for this reason and have been contacted by email many times by newly diagnosed PALS trying to deal with, cope, and accept their fate. Another ideal way to talk among others who have been through the same emotions is through an online ALS chat room. Here you can get real time suggestions to very personal issues from many different perspectives. The chat room I frequently visit has as many as a dozen PALS present all in different phases of paralysis. The support from these online friends can be significant.

To move on means accepting the cards you're dealt however distasteful and unpleasant. It means not letting yourself be completely consumed by the tragedy, rather ALS should be viewed as an irritating parasite that you must learn to live with. If you refuse to accept simply means accepting heartache, sorrow, and despair. Instead, by being informed and supported, you can learn to accept the imposition of something as devastating as ALS. This familiar short prayer describes very well our choice to accept—"God, grant me the serenity to accept the things I cannot change, the courage to change the things I can, and the wisdom to know the difference." (Reinhold Niebuhr)

I have talked to many people who have told me they can accept they have ALS but they could never live with tubes. This is refusing to adapt. The truth about ALS is that eventually you will need a feeding tube, a BiPap, and maybe a ventilator, without them you simply accept death without adjusting to the reality of the disease. Technology today has made these lifesaving interventions available in-home and easy to use. Personal views about using or not using current technology readily available to us can be complicated and emotional. It brings to mind a short story told during a sermon in my home church many years before I was diagnosed with ALS but its message was strong and I always remembered it. It is paraphrased here.

"During a particularly rainy season, there were threats of floods. As a man stood on his porch, a police car with a bullhorn drove by saying 'You must evacuate, there will be severe floods.' But the man didn't evacuate, he thought 'The Lord will keep me safe.' As the rain continued and the water rose, he was forced to move to his second floor. A boat came to him and a rescuer called out, 'Get in the boat, we can save you.' But the man refused, he thought 'The Lord will keep me safe.' The rain continued and the man had to move to the roof. A helicopter came and the rescuers said, 'Climb the rope ladder, we can save you.' Again the man refused, he thought 'The Lord will keep me safe.' The rain continued and the man was swept to his death. Later when this man stood before the Lord in heaven, he asked the question that troubled him. 'Lord, I have been a God-fearing man, I have followed your Word. Why did You allow me to die so early?' The Lord answered, 'I sent you a police car, a boat, and a helicopter but you didn't listen.'"

The message to me is clear regarding its relevance to ALS. Man has been given intelligence, curiosity, and compassion to help others. Tremendous advances in medical technology have occurred in just the past 50 years. For example, we now routinely use mechanical heart valves to correct cardiac valvular disease; organ transplants occur daily to give new life to those previously with no hope of living; blood transfusions are commonplace. If we fail to adapt to what medicine has to offer each day, we would be stuck in the dark ages. As the man who refused the help that was available in the flood, some also will refuse medical help and won't listen or acknowledge today's technology intended not only to improve quality of life but survival itself.

Regarding living with "tubes," I say be informed, do your research, and talk to others who use them. Make rationale decisions based on fact not emotion. For me, having to use a feeding tube is equivalent to the need for glasses for some people. Sure, you can do without it but why make yourself miserable.

Adapting though is more than tubes, it's also adapting to a new lifestyle. Living in the past and constantly reliving "what ifs" serves no purpose except to pull you deeper into despair. When it's time for a wheelchair, be thankful for the means to be mobile. When it's time for a feeding tube, be thankful for the means to eat without choking. When it's time to allow strangers to be your caregivers, be thankful such people have caring hearts. When your voice is gone, be thankful for voice synthesizers and voice banking. Instead of being stubborn and refusing the help available, turn it around by graciously adapting to your changing situation and maybe invent a few novel approaches to the inevitable obstacles that arise. For example when I could no longer use a straw to rinse my mouth after having my teeth brushed that meant I had to contrive something that met my needs. Now I use two spray bottles, one with water, one with mouthwash. It worked for me. I adapted.

Attitude is everything. How many times have we heard this? A positive approach influences all we do. A right attitude though is neither overly optimistic nor depressingly pessimistic, rather it is a balanced healthy view of your situation. For example, instead of seeing the glass half full or half empty, simply be thankful for the glass. It's a different perspective but effective.

When my attitude needs adjustment, I have found a valuable source of inspiration in reading how others have lived their lives under less than ideal circumstances. One of the most powerful is Victor Frankl's account of survival as a Jew in Hitler's death camps in Man's Search For Meaning. But I am also inspired by one of our greatest U. S. Presidents, Franklin Delano Roosevelt, who was elected to an unprecedented four terms while a paraplegic in a wheelchair due to polio. His story from this perspective is told in FDR's Splendid Deception. Many more books are available to enlighten, offer a different point of view, and pull us out of a self-induced pity. I have listed some of these books at the end of this book. Another present day inspiration is British professor Stephen Hawking, a ventilator dependent quadriplegic due to ALS for more than 40 years, who has changed the world's thinking about astrophysics. Though he doesn't write about his disability, he has written many books about the theories of the universe including his famous A Brief History of Time and The Universe in a Nutshell. He has refused to sink into a self-pitying passive attitude of nothingness, rather he works and makes important contributions toward our understanding of space. His example of living with his disability serves as an important model when we feel like we can't or don't want to live with its current challenges.

Another way I keep my attitude in check is to "talk" with my friend Dave using IM (instant messaging). Dave is my ALS friend, about my same age who is also a ventilator dependent quadriplegic. Having a close friend with ALS is so important mainly because nobody can truly understand the intricate emotions that sometimes consume us. I once asked Dave, what is the difference between all the people with ALS who die after just a few years and people like us who are in our second decade? His answer was simple. He said we are ornery. And we laughed.

ALS may take our physical body but it can't take our mind or attitude. Consider this thought-provoking Russian parable, which I have paraphrased.

Two frogs were hopping along when they happened to jump into a large container of whipped cream. They jumped, kicked, and struggled but they kept sinking in the whipped cream. It was like quicksand. Finally, one frog said, "If I am going to die anyway, I am just going to stop struggling now." He stopped his efforts and quickly perished. The other frog said, "If I am going to die, I want to die fighting." So he kicked and kicked. Slowly the whipped cream changed to butter and the frog jumped to safety.

Which frog are you? Is your attitude to give up and die or to fight and survive?

The last part of my formula to be a survivor, after accepting, adapting, and checking your attitude, is aggressively pursuing your ambitions. Whatever they may be, whatever is important to you, these ambitions help you feel productive, useful to your family or community, and satisfied with yourself. As you lose more and more physical movement, a computer will become your best friend and help you realize these ambitions. Technology today has allowed computers to do just about anything our minds can dream up, we are limited only by our own imagination. So figure out what you want to do then figure out how to make it happen. If you feel stuck, read how others have made their ambitions a reality, like FDR, Stephen Hawking, and Christopher Reeve.

I am often amazed with the technology available today that wasn't imaginable just ten years ago. I wonder how Lou Gehrig would have taken advantage of what we have today. Ubiquitous email has replaced handwritten letters. Instant messaging has replaced phone calls. Webex software allows active participation in conference calls. Voice synthesizers speak typed words. And so much more. By asking the right questions of the right people you can discover a whole new world of possibilities that is only increasing everyday. All this technology benefits the disabled tremendously. For those who say they are not computer savvy, there is no better time to learn than now.

Martin Luther King Jr. once said, "Our lives begin to end the day we become silent about things that matter." The disabled have a voice as loud as anyone else but it must be used to be heard. Instead of sitting back and complaining about this or that, do something about it. I have always been one to see a problem and do something to make it better. Sometimes we see issues from a slightly different perspective because of our circumstances. Use that to our advantage. For example, Christopher Reeve raised awareness about spinal cord injury research and established the Christopher Reeve Paralysis Foundation. President Roosevelt proved to be formidable with his paralysis and established the March of Dimes. Stephen Hawking brought attention to his disability when he recently experienced weightlessness in a highly publicized zero gravity flight. But closer to home, you and I also have the power to impact things "that matter" whether it's raising money for research or writing your congressional representatives to support legislation that impacts you or improving your personal care. This is what I mean by aggressively pursuing your ambitions, whatever they may be. By being actively involved and engaged in something that matters not only makes you feel satisfied and content but also positively impacts those around you.

It all boils down to finding your niche in a new lifestyle. Getting stuck in reverse is destructive, that is living in the past. When something catastrophic, unexpected, life-changing happens, it's not the end of the world, unless of course you want it to be. Have a serious talk with yourself about how you want to proceed and cover the issues of acceptance, adjustment, the right attitude, and identification of your personal ambitions. Then simply do it.

Appendix A ALS Resources

This is a list of online resources I have personally found helpful.

ALS Association
www.alsa.org
27001 Agoura Road, Suite 150
Calabasas Hills, CA 91301–5104
818–880–9007

Muscular Dystrophy Association's ALS Division
www.als-mda.org
National Headquarters
3300 E. Sunrise Drive
Tucson, AZ 85718
800–344–4863

ALS Therapy Development Institute (TDI)
www.als.net
215 First Street
Cambridge, MA 02142
617–441–7200

ALS Chat Room
http://client1.sigmachat.com/sc.php?id=144320

ALS Message Board
BrainTalk Communities: Online Patient Support Group
http://brain.hastypastry.net/forums/forumdisplay.php?f=8
2

Information on Clinical Trials and Human Research
Studies
A service of the US National Institutes of Health
clinicaltrials.gov.

International Ventilator Users Network (IVUN)
ventusers.org
4207 Lindell Blvd, #110
Saint Louis, MO 63108–2930
314–534–0475

ALS Research at Johns Hopkins—Packard Center
alscenter.org
5801 Smith Avenue / McAuley Suite 110
Baltimore, MD 21209–3652

Appendix B Recommended Reading

These books are intended to inspire and motivate. None are about ALS.

FDR's Splendid Deception
By Hugh Gregory Gallagher
The 32nd U.S. president contracted polio as a young man yet overcame the obstacles of paraplegia to lead our nation during harrowing times from a wheelchair.

Man's Search For Meaning
By Viktor Frankl
A psychiatrist discusses his experiences at Auschwitz during World War II and offers explanations for why some people survived such severe adversity.

Nothing Is Impossible: Reflections On a New Life
By Christopher Reeve
The superman actor challenges readers not to accept limitations but harness untapped resources within themselves.

The Impossible Just Takes a Little Longer: Living With Purpose and Passion
By Art Berg
A quadriplegic becomes a motivational speaker and imparts lessons about life, fear, and passion.

The Purpose-Driven Life: What On Earth Am I Here For?
By Richard Warren
A Baptist pastor helps readers discover, develop, and fulfill God's purpose for their lives.

When Bad Things Happen To Good People
By Harold S. Kushner
A Jewish rabbi offers thoughtful answers to poignant questions after his young son is diagnosed with a fatal disease.

Who Moved My Cheese?
By Spencer Johnson
A management expert tells a parable about adapting to change.

LaVergne, TN USA
03 February 2010
171914LV00002B/39/P